BUCK PETERSON'S

COMPLETE GUIDE TO
BIRD HUNTING

BUCK PETERSON'S
COMPLETE GUIDE TO
BIRD HUNTING

BY
BUCK "BUCK" PETERSON

ILLUSTRATIONS BY
J. ANGUS "SOURDOUGH" MCLEAN

TEN SPEED PRESS
Berkeley | Toronto

Copyright © 2007 by Buck "Buck" Peterson

All rights reserved. No part of this book may be reproduced in any form without the written permission of the publisher, except in the case of brief quotations embodied in critical articles or reviews. Many of the designations used by manufacturers and sellers to distinguish their products are claimed as trademarks. Where the publisher is aware of a trademark claim, such designations, in this book, have initial capital letters.
The choice of ink color should not be construed as signifying that Buck is "going green."

Ten Speed Press
PO Box 7123
Berkeley, California 94707
www.tenspeed.com

Distributed in Australia by Simon and Schuster Australia, in Canada by Ten Speed Press Canada, in New Zealand by Southern Publishers Group, in South Africa by Real Books, and in the United Kingdom and Europe by Publishers Group UK.

Cover design by Betsy Stromberg
Interior design by Headcase Design, Philadelphia, PA
Interior production by Michael Cutter
Illustrations by J. Angus "Sourdough" McLean

Library of Congress Cataloging-in-Publication Data

Peterson, B. R.
Buck Peterson's complete guide to bird hunting / by Buck "Buck" Peterson ; illustrations by J. Angus "Sourdough" McLean.
p. cm.
ISBN 978-1-58008-739-1
1. Hunting—Humor. 2. Fowling—Humor. I. Title.
PN6231.H77P47 2007
818'.5402—dc22
2007008363

Printed in Canada
First printing, 2007

1 2 3 4 5 6 7 8 9 10 — 11 10 09 08 07

THE ROGUES GALLERY ANSWER KEY

1–C
2–A
3–B
4–F
5–D
6–E

DEDICATION

This bird-hunting book is dedicated to the caged pet birds who will never know the joys of flying free, riding the thermals, soaring, diving, thinking world peace, flitting in and out of the range of Buck's shotgun. And to the missed game birds of a Minnesota youth and questionable adulthood. They know who they are, the cheeky bastards.

DISCLAIMER: Information contained in this guidebook has been vetted by respected ornithologists, one retired gynecologist with advanced tunnel vision, and the happy hour regulars of Buck's Valhalla Lounge. The editorial review of the wild turkey section was accompanied with supersized portions of a similarly named adult beverage. In the future, the author promises to drink more responsibly and, more importantly, to cover the dog's ears when shooting turkeys out the truck window. Finally, products mentioned in the text were not paid for by their manufacturers. Not that they weren't asked.

MEDICAL ALERT: Upland birds exploding at your feet or a sky full of greenheads with cupped wings can be hazardous to your health. See Emergency First Aid—Cardiac Arrest.

CONTENTS

INTRODUCTION IX

THE MOST FREQUENTLY ASKED QUESTIONS ABOUT BIRDS AND BIRD HUNTING X

THE HUNTED 1
The Bird World / Game Birds / Key Differences between Domestic and Wild Birds / Key Bird Senses and Activities / Migrations / Buck's Bonus Tips

HUNTING EQUIPMENT 13
Shotguns / The Case for Truck Guns / Shotgun Shells / Nontoxic Ammunition: Getting the Lead Out / Safety Equipment / Bird Decoys / Confidence Decoys / Blinds / Bird Dogs / More Buck's Bonus Tips

HUNTING TECHNIQUES: GENERAL 37
The Ten Commandments of Firearm Safety / Master Eye / Trap Shooting / Skeet Shooting / Sporting Clays / Patterning / Wind as a Shooting Variable / Shooting Etiquette / Summary of Regulations / Government Hunting / Face Camouflage / Hunting on Private Land / Hunting on Public Land / Hunting in Canada, Argentina, and Mexico

HUNTING TECHNIQUES: UPLAND BIRDS 69
Practice / Clothing / Birdcalls / Pointing Dogs / Don't Shoot! / A Bird Dog's Self-Esteem / Hunting in Snake Country / How to Age and Sex an Upland Game Bird / The Different Kinds / The Problem

HUNTING TECHNIQUES: WATERFOWL 109
Clothing / Decoy Patterns / Hunting in Rivers and Oceans / Wild Goose Chase / Retrieving Crippled Ducks / Hunting Late-Season Waterfowl / Still More Buck's Bonus Tips / The Different Kinds

FROM FIELD TO TABLE 139
Bird Care / At the End of the Day / Contract Bird Cleaning / Bird Cleaning in Motel Rooms / Transporting the Birds / Table / Recipes

MISCELLANEOUS 163
The Second Collection of the Most Frequently Asked Questions about Birds and Bird Hunting / Coots Unlimited and Forevermore / Bird Banding / A Flock of Contemporary Business Lessons / Guide to Tipping / Grand-Slam Bird Hunting / Inconvenient Truths / Holiday Gifts

ABRIDGED AFTERWORD 176

UNABRIDGED AFTERWORD 177

APPENDIX: BIRDBRAINED QUOTATIONS 178

INTRODUCTION

Waterfowling was my first bird-hunting passion in north-central Minnesota. There weren't many ducks—and fewer geese—at the margins of the Central flyway, but friends and family hunted out of seventeen-foot-square-stern fiberglass Herter canoes and over hand-carved wood decoys, hand-painted according to George's explicit instructions. We knew pheasants and sage grouse and quail and snow geese and turkeys and doves and sandhill cranes lived elsewhere in the world but, on our little pond, we were in no hurry to go elsewhere. Now that my hunting has included an often hard-earned share of "elsewhere" birds, I am again in no hurry to get more or go elsewhere, and I still prefer a little pond with friends and family. The Winchester Model 50 I bought as a teen is back in use with the new, more powerful nontoxic loads. When it jams, it's okay, because there is no better "jam" than time in the field, savoring clear and cloudy days with brightly colored, wild birds in full flight and an old lab (or hunting pig) that is just as happy with a one- or no-bird day.

THE MOST FREQUENTLY ASKED QUESTIONS ABOUT BIRDS AND BIRD HUNTING

1. *My bird dog's food looks, smells, and tastes better than anything my mother-in-law cooks.*
   Mine too.

2. *Do you have to ask permission from the folks in the farmhouse to shoot pheasants in their front yard?*
   Not always. In Vermont, for example, you don't have to ask if the bathroom light is the only one on inside the house. If you can see the widow lady at the kitchen window, stop in for a piece of pie.

3. *Is Mr. Peanut salted in the shell?*
   I'd check with his missus if she wasn't such a nutcase.

4. *My wife starts foaming at the mouth every time I mention a new shotgun. Should I get shots for rabies?*
   Yes.

5. *We housewives in my cul-de-sac get goose bumps just thinking of you in the cul-de-sack, if you know what I mean, you big lug.*
   I do not find this a moral impasse.

6. *If there was no gravity, would birds still fall from the sky?*
   Yes, but they would fall up.

THE MOST FREQUENTLY ASKED QUESTIONS

7. *I know this question should be in your deer-hunting guide, but I missed the deadline. How often do does have antlers?*
   One estimate is 1 in 35,000 cases—about the same percentage as women with mustaches. Church barbers in the convent report an average of one mustache per every ten nuns, or a full beard per every mother superior.

8. *Do you have Prince Albert in the can?*
   Sure smells like it. I do have Aunt Jemima in a very squeezable bottle. And I sure do enjoy Mrs. Field's cookie.

9. *My brother-in-law just bought a house in a development called Quail Run, but there aren't any quail out there.*
   They sure gave him a run for his money.

10. *Buck, you no-good, sleazy bastard. What did you put in my drink, anyway? I had to throw my best panties away. Expect a call from my lawyer. P.S. Your twins say hello.*
    Sorry, wrong number.

THE HUNTED

THE BIRD WORLD

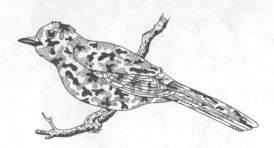

DEFINITIONS

BIRD: **1:** Any of various warm-blooded, egg-laying, feathered, winged vertebrates; **2:** An obscene gesture.

EARLY BIRD: Any such winged vertebrate that gets the worm *and* an obscene gesture from others in the warm, comfortable nest.

GAME BIRD: Any such winged vertebrate that is hunted for sport.

FAIR GAME: A game bird that is not able to return fire.

Which leads to. . . .

LIFE IS NOT FAIR

A bird's first life lesson is this: life is not fair. Our understanding of the bird world is limited to our history and our most immediate surroundings. Youngsters are awakened by bluebirds of happiness; watch cartoon birds like Tweety foil Sylvester the cat's natural ambitions on the Cartoon History

Channel, and, in the Heartland, wonder why only New York City had huge, freakish yellow birds living down the street. Then they grow up to be adult bird fanciers, checking off life lists and cheering up with the sight of the first robin of spring.

On close examination, however, all is not in balance in the bird world. Park pigeons are demanding five-grain bread crumbs; red-tailed hawks are taking up free residence outside exclusive condominiums; and the orange sauce on Hooters wings stains the most impervious fabric. Crows aggressively and noisily guard parking lot dumpsters; starling nests jam chimneys and dryer vents; seagulls scatter their white, chalky droppings on our favorite seaside vacation spots; and cardinals in the Mother Church still insist on fish-stick Fridays.

Avian influenza is the latest apocalyptic warning, no surprise to those who see a host of avian diseases—including histoplasmosis, cryptococcus, and salmonella—piled high on equestrian statues in many parks. Avian flu occurs naturally in wild birds, and now strains of this disease threaten the bird world. In recent years an Asian strain of this disease has spread across Africa, Asia, and Europe, killing thousands of birds. Several governments slaughtered millions of infected domestic poultry, causing the price of extra-crispy chicken strips to skyrocket.

This bird flu hasn't appeared in North America yet. You can protect yourself and those you care about against this bird disease, along with whooping cough and miscellaneous birdbrained social dysfunctions, by following these practical guidelines:

✔ Give birds that look sick to others in your hunting party.

✔ Do not lick your fingers while cleaning birds.

✔ Wear a condom while plucking birds.

✔ Don't use duck or goose fat as a skin moisturizer.

✔ Let your wife's cat clean your working surfaces.

✔ Cook your meat to 165 degrees (or less, if you like it rare).

These largely urban fears are not, however, spreading to the countryside, where the original balance of nature is restored by well-meaning carnivores.

GAME BIRDS

Game birds are birds hunted for food (migrating urban birds are reminded of their first life lesson; see "Life Is Not Fair," page 2). Domesticated game birds are not easily found except on preserves, where they should be dispatched with extreme prejudice; prematurely expired ex-urban birds should be left out in the yard for the barn cats.

Bird hunting is a sport anchored in our nation's early history—once it was freed from the game-hogging British royals and other Eurotrash. At the first Thanksgiving, Pilgrims had a lick of the abundant game in the new country and, relying on Native Americans to provide the holiday meal, set the stage for a welfare system favored by the New World Democratic Party. The more self-reliant emigrants headed west to hunt in the Central and Pacific flyways, and pioneering Scandinavians arrived in northern Minnesota after a long voyage through the Great Lakes. Unfortunately, the barrels of salted cod also survived the journey; fortunately, their survival jump-started the Swedish meatball industry in our country. Game birds were a staple in our earliest diets; while many early recipes were lost in the moves, seniors today recall larders full of loons, eagles, carrier pigeons, and, at family reunions, an occasional dodo.

The large family of American game birds presents the modern bird hunter with unique opportunities to pursue traditional field sports. In the post–September 11 world, a new guidebook is a relevant and well-meaning public service. Homeland security should never be far from a patriotic bird hunter's attention, considering the seditious thoughts carried by border-crossing Francophile honkers from Quebec.

KEY DIFFERENCES BETWEEN DOMESTIC AND WILD BIRDS

Turkeys are a perfect example for illustrating the major differences between a "hothouse" domestic bird and a wild-as-the-wind game bird.

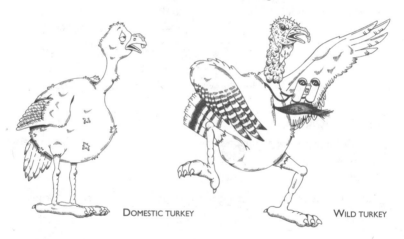

Domestic turkey   Wild turkey

PHYSICAL APPEARANCE

The domestic turkey has the muscle tone of an ordinary office worker. They can't move quickly and are easy targets for urban predators, as seen on *Law & Order/Avian CSI*. Domestic turkeys are raised to enjoy confined spaces and rely on a predictable handout of processed food. Their feathers are a bland white, and gender differences aren't obvious until you turn them upside down—and even then you need to know what to look for. Through genetic manipulation, their white-meat breasts are large and, in the factory, they don't mind having their belly button replaced by a red button. They also don't mind being prestuffed with old bread chunks (and they still taste like chicken).

Wild turkeys, on the other hand, are smart, aggressive, and quick-witted avian athletes. Their alert senses and innate caution protect them from all predators but Buck. Surviving their brutish habitat makes them tough, but it's nothing that a dip in hot oil out on the deck can't cure. Gender differences are obvious, and wild turkeys are good role models for their young. Compared to a domestic turkey, wild tom turkeys are as reticent as a Texas ranger. And wild-turkey meat reflects a truly all-natural, organic, free-range diet of acorns, berries, grains, seeds, insects, and the occasional peanut butter and jelly sandwich left behind by a frustrated nonresident hunter. And wild turkeys are disease free compared to domestic birds, which suffer from common urban ailments such as whooping cough, gingivitis, and avian attention deficit disorder. And if you don't think the advantages of a wild life computes in that bird brain of theirs, look more closely: wild turkeys smile more.

HISTORICAL NOTE: Ben Franklin preferred the wild turkey over the bald eagle for a national symbol. Historians think this preference arose from a taste test in his backyard.

BUCK'S DUH TIP: What liquor company would use a domestic turkey as a brand symbol?

KEY BIRD SENSES AND ACTIVITIES

SENSES

With few exceptions (most notably, wild turkeys), game birds share similar senses, unless they are in the past tense.

TOUCH: Rigor mortis sets in on a wild bird upon field dressing. You are a soft touch if the in-laws get the first pick of the birds at the end of the day.

SMELL: Game birds smell real good—if they aren't field-dressed and carried in your warm game pouch all day.

HEARING: Game birds hear at the lower frequencies of sound, while bird dogs hear at the highest frequencies. High-frequency contact between the two is the goal.

SIGHT: Eyes on the sides of the head allow a game bird to see your shiny face in a wide-screen format.

TASTE: Game birds taste good—unless their diet is asparagus. This is yet another reason not to eat asparagus or, for that matter, broccoli or cauliflower.

ACTIVITIES

WALKING: Migratory game birds walk with difficulty with good reason: their legs are spaced like those of an elderly upland-bird hunter with a load in his pants. Nonmigratory geese and ducks that have created avian toilets in places like

urban parks and golf courses, however, easily wobble from one picnic basket to another—one more reason to hand them their ass when the park closes.

FLYING: Migratory game birds fly because they cannot walk fast enough. The only other option for birds to get to their winter grounds is to take public transportation, but with the cutbacks in Greyhound service, there is no inexpensive, direct route from Canada to Mexico anymore. Buses now service only urban centers in the most dangerous parts of town, and their personnel are not used to dealing with waterfowl that want to put tickets on their bills. Trains are no better—their best routes are east-west. With the "birds of a feather" rate now discontinued, commercial air travel is out of the question.

Nonmigratory game birds fly to avoid ground sluices. Upland birds like to run, and that's why pheasant legs are worth saving. An honest coyote would admit that pheasant legs are much better tasting than turkey legs. Upland birds have feathered legs, which no self-respecting duck would tolerate.

MIGRATIONS

Game birds migrate for two reasons: to get somewhere else, and to qualify for federal protection. Like midwestern snowbirds, waterfowl travel long distances, heading south for the winter and returning in the spring. Unlike midwestern snowbirds, waterfowl head south to have sex in tropical settings and return to lay their eggs in Canada. Upland birds are built for short, often flightless travel; for many, this is reason enough to shoot them where they stand, especially chukars.

DUCKS

Four waterfowl flyways—Pacific, Central, Mississippi, and Atlantic—were established in 1948 to designate the migration routes of ducks and the duck hunters who follow them. Information on the latter is particularly helpful to beer distributors.

The flyway boundaries between the Central and the Mississippi, and between the Mississippi and the Atlantic flyways follow state lines, while the boundary between the Central and the Pacific flyways generally follow the Continental Divide, also known as the Great Divide. The divide roughly follows the Rocky Mountains and separates the major watersheds that flow west to the Pacific from those that flow north to the Arctic Ocean or east to the Atlantic Ocean (including those via the Gulf of Mexico). Any water left over is bottled as a beverage that goes well with beer nuts.

Each flyway differs in species composition, number of each species, and origin of breeding ground. The rather arbitrary boundaries do not prevent some species from crossing east-west boundaries. A duck's internal compass, originally set to magnetic north, may be compromised by steel shot under its skullcap.

GEESE

Two general geese flyways are recognized for the population management of Canada geese: those that cross over private golf courses, and those that cross over public golf courses. From their altitude, however, honkers can't distinguish ownership and focus on the nearest open green.

Migrations along the two flyways are interrupted by short-stopping on public and private beaches, city parks, and any other grassy urban space near water where children play.

THE BEST REASON TO HUNT WILD GAME BIRDS: THE CANADA GOOSE

To our vast urban population, the Canada goose is the symbol of the wild kingdom. Honkers moving from pond to park, or those on semiannual migrations have the ability to give pause to pedestrians and motorists alike. Even nannies in the park are delighted to share grassy knolls with these magnificent winged creatures. That is, until the true nature of the Canada goose is revealed.

In our new global village, toxic waste management is the responsibility of every American citizen. And the call to arms is predictably covered under the 2nd, 5th, 8th, and 69th Amendments.

BUCK'S BONUS TIPS

✔ If you are sleeping in a bunkhouse or sharing a motel room with others, problem snorers can be silenced with firm pressure on a feather pillow, or with duct tape applied liberally once the handcuffs are secured to the bedpost.

✔ If you get lost while wandering from camp at night to take care of some personal business, lie down faceup and line up an object with a star. This star will move from this object in a westerly direction, except when the Big Dipper is below Polaris, Yamaha, or Suzuki.

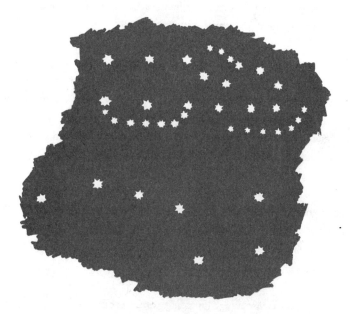

✔ If you get lost on the open prairie, remember that the sun sets in the west (if it is not cloudy). More people live out east, though, so your likelihood of running into someone by heading east is greater.

✔ If you get confused in a cornfield, corn is planted in rows, so just follow the ruts. Sometimes corn is planted in crop circles on uneven terrain, though, so unless you like corn for all three meals, prepare to die in the maize maze.

✔ The very best upland bird–hunting lodges offer cognac and cigars after dinner. The preferred after-dinner entertainment for corporate heads is Mr. Potato Head. Bring your own game box to be safe. The kitchen has extra russets.

✔ When hunting in flooded timber, the higher you sit in the tree, the more ducks you will shoot before other hunters. Don't shoot lower than a horizontal plane, unless you enjoy ducking yourself.

✔ To shoot a double or triple, first pick out a bird in the back of the flock, and then work your way forward. If you shoot the same bird twice, international sporting clays rules allow you to claim a modified double. If you shoot a double with a single-barreled shotgun, you owe yourself a double-barreled shotgun. If you shoot a triple with a double-barreled shotgun, tell your boss to get screwed.

✔ Old, beat-up decoys can enjoy another season with you in the boat if you cut the bodies in half and mount them on the side of your duck boat. Make sure you mount the left side of the decoy on the left side of the boat so it'll look like the birds are swimming forward. Game birds rarely swim backwards unless they know you will shoot them on the water.

✔ Flock shooting is discouraged in polite company, but it is acceptable behavior when the Homeland Security threat level is orange or higher.

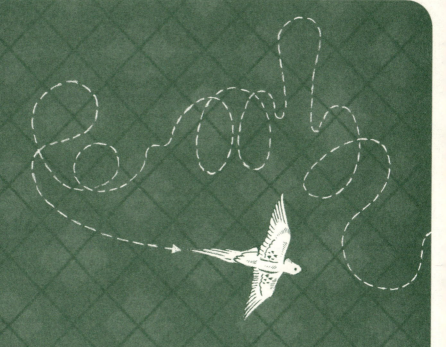

HUNTING EQUIPMENT

SHOTGUNS

Dear Buck: How do you know when you have too much gun?
When you close your eyes before pulling the trigger. Note that except in Wisconsin, it is against the law to shoot what you can't see.

Generally speaking, you must use a shotgun to shoot game birds—unless you are shooting eagles for ceremonial feathers, or you have a silencer for your handgun. Shotguns are separated by design and function. By design, bird guns come with one or two barrels.

SINGLE-BARRELED SHOTGUNS

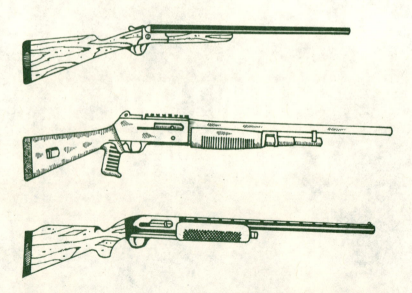

Semiautomatic shotguns have the ability to shoot more than one shot quickly, just by pulling the trigger. This type of action is favored by SWAT teams everywhere, which should tell you something. These shotguns are preferred for flock-shooting. Semiautomatics are either gas operated or inertia driven, and the marketing gas for both mechanisms causes great buyer inertia.

Pump shotguns are often called "trombones" by detractors because the action is pumped to inject another shell before firing. Pump-action shotguns, however, have brought more birds to bag than any other firearm, especially during pheasant season in the Dakotas.

Single-shot shotguns are the most reliable and least costly of single-barreled shotguns. Very fast hands are required to shoot doubles and triples with this firearm—unless the birds are still in the nest.

DOUBLE-BARRELED SHOTGUNS

Over-under shotguns have one barrel atop another, much like you and your spouse at night when things are going great guns. The shooting plane on an over-under is the same as a single-barreled shotgun, but you have a backup barrel in case you missed your attorney with the first round.

Under-over shotguns have a similar configuration, but with the trigger guard on top. These shotguns are most easily fired when hanging upside down in a tree-stand safety harness.

Side-by-side shotguns have barrels lying side by side, much like you and your spouse when things are going just OK.

A traditionalist's favorite, the side-by-side shotgun is unavailable in modern composite or composite-and-camouflage stocks.

BUCK'S BONUS TIP: Wood stocks, however, are much easier to notch.

SHOTGUN SPECS

STOCKS: Walnut is considered to be the finest wood for shotgun stocks, and farmers in Illinois guard their walnut trees more closely than they do their daughters. English walnut is lighter than Turkish walnut, but then again Turkish food is at least edible.

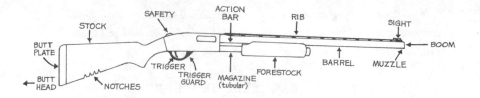

GRIPS: Straight stocks are more common on double-barreled shotguns owned by those who already have a grip on things.

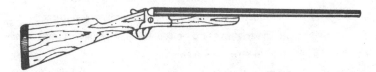

Pistol grips are for those shooters who need to pistol-whip wild birds, while purists insist that a pistol grip is one you must be able to get your thumb around.

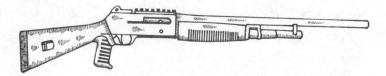

Less pure shooters can use a modified pistol grip.

A Prince of Wales grip is a distinguished, rounded "heel" named after the vestigial tail common to inbred royal families of Europe. This tail will eventually disappear as royals marry more commoners.

TRIGGERS: Buyers have a choice of single or double triggers in fine side-by-side or over-under shotguns. The advantage of a double trigger is two chokes to respond to changing field situations. For example, if you see a family of no-goods stealing your watermelons, you'll want a loose choke to spray the whole rotten bunch of them, but while riding shotgun on a jailhouse chain-gang, try a tight choke for focused knock-down power. Americans buy mostly single-triggered shotguns because, in states other than Alabama, Arkansas, and Mississippi, prisoners on a chain gang can no longer be shot within fifty yards of a public thoroughfare. Europeans, on the other hand, still prefer double triggers—except for the Germans, who prefer single-trigger semi- and fully automatic firearms when dealing with the French.

GAUGES: The bore diameter of a shotgun barrel is referred to as gauge. Based on an old British measurement system, the measure is certainly not exact; it calculates the number of lead balls of the same bore diameter required to make up one pound of lead balls. For example, a 12-gauge bore will hold a lead ball weighing one-twelfth of a pound. Given the instability of the English pound, your gauge changes daily, which is another reason to own more shotguns. You'll need them to accurately fit changing field conditions.

Recoil measured in foot-pounds of energy increases with gauge sizes. A 28-gauge over-under shotgun would only hurt a pocketbook, while a 10-gauge would discourage your wife from sharing your favorite field sports (not a bad thing). Felt recoil is artificially measured in comfort levels for sensitive shooters.

> **BUCK'S SHOOTING TIP:** Flinching indicates an improperly held shotgun, a shotgun that's too large, a shotshell load that's too heavy, or a history of being hit in the head by a spouse or floor supervisor. In the last case, this is another reason to fake a kidnapping and catch a tramp steamer to New Zealand.

CHOKES: Muzzle constriction affects shot patterns (see "Patterning," page 50) and shotguns come with a variety of choke inserts. No choke at the muzzle is called a cylinder bore, for use on preserve birds, in watermelon patches, and for unplanned weddings. More disciplined shot patterns exit via improved cylinders and modified chokes. A full-bore choke is best for long-range sky carp and small turkey heads. Large turkey heads are best removed with a special turkey choke hold.

> **BUCK'S BONUS TIP:** Firearm choke manufacturers have a padded room off the factory floor where new ideas can be discussed without interruption. And with great mirth. Predictions for the upcoming season: "Only Slightly Modified," "New and Improved," and "Under New Management" chokes.

SHOTGUNS BY SPECIES

Upland-bird hunters typically hunt small upland birds with double-barreled shotguns in the smaller 16, 20, and 26 gauges, with 20 being the most popular. Large-game bird hunters insist on a minimum 12-gauge shotgun—10 for golf-course honkers. Upland-bird guns differ most from waterfowl shotguns in other, often cosmetic ways.

SHOTGUN DESIGN BY SPECIES

UPLAND BIRDS	WATERFOWL
Fancy walnut stocks	Pressed-wood, laminated-wood, or composite stocks
Fine receiver engravings	Model number and manufacturer warnings on barrel
Checkered-wood butt plates	6"–12" recoil pads

BUCK'S BONUS TIP: Double-barreled shotguns have four grades of shell removal: grade one—you remove the shell case with a pair of pliers; grade two—shot shells are slightly extracted so you can remove easily; grade three—shells are ejected; grade four—your porter removes the shell husks. Single-barreled semiautomatics have one grade of shell removal: warp speed.

THEIR FIRST SHOTGUN

FOR A YOUNG LAD OR LASS: Single-shot or pump-action, 20-gauge shotguns are mechanically easy to understand and the safest to operate. Shorter gun stocks are available in the "youth" category, as are light-load shells, which reduce recoil.

FOR A WIFE: If your spouse is small, a youth gun will suffice. If she balks at this category, tell her it makes her look more youthful. If you sleep with a large woman, this is a golden opportunity to unload or replace an old shotgun. If you sleep with a really large woman, with a little camouflage cloth, she might make a good duck-and-turkey blind. If she sleeps with a really large man, then, using a ghillie suit, you can become your own blind.

BUCK'S BONUS TIP: **If you sleep on the couch with any regularity, remove firing pins from all firearms.**

THE CASE FOR TRUCK GUNS

With the exception of hunting guides and competition shooters, there are as many game birds knocked down with a truck gun as with something nice and shiny sitting in the gun cabinet. These specialty shotguns are stored behind the truck's front seat, in the cab of the combine, in a corner of the milk shed, or, if operational, on the gun rack in the truck's back window. There is no case for a truck gun. The dog most likely ate it.

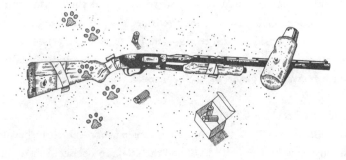

IDENTIFYING MARKS

RUST: Grades one (new) to five (deep pitted and well earned).

SIGHTS: Front bead missing; rib bent or missing.

SCOPE: Only the mounts remain from last year's deer hunt.

STOCK: Made of particleboard, a composite of sawdust; if the stock is broken at the comb, it is duct-taped together. Or bolted.

HUNTING EQUIPMENT

SEMIAUTOMATIC: With a one-shot capability—even if it's a pump, which is more likely.

MANUFACTURER: Unknown, or unable to identify.

MULTIPLE USES

✔ Pull in duck decoys by hooking the string with the shotgun's barrel.

✔ Knock down hunting gear from high shelves.

✔ Paddle your boat.

✔ Most importantly, use it as an emergency homeland security avian control device on a Sunday drive in the countryside.

SHOTGUN SHELLS

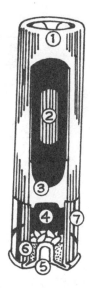

Shotgun shells used in bird hunting share design elements and ingredients.

STANDARD

1. Tube or container made of plastic or paper that explodes in many directions with heavy hand-loads.

2. Shot that breaks the flesh of game birds and, if steel shot, dental caps. (Nonresident shells have no shot; see figure.)

3. Wad from the phrase "shot your wad."

4. Powder that explodes, sending forth wad and shot to miss a game bird.

5. Primer that is struck by the firearm's firing pin to start noisy explosion above.

6. Base wad used by those who have an overabundance of wad.

7. Head is the shiny, metal end cap, opposite the only end that is supposed to explode unless your shells are really old with rusted heads.

NONRESIDENT

Nonresident shells are easily identified by their low powder and absence of shot. Upland-bird shotgun shells differ from waterfowl shells, most notably in size.

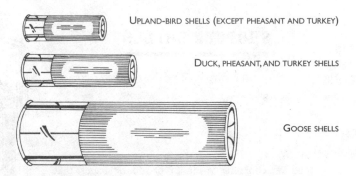

UPLAND-BIRD SHELLS (EXCEPT PHEASANT AND TURKEY)

DUCK, PHEASANT, AND TURKEY SHELLS

GOOSE SHELLS

NONTOXIC AMMUNITION: GETTING THE LEAD OUT

Lead shot has been shown to cause lead poisoning in a variety of birds, especially waterfowl, and nontoxic ammunition has been required for all waterfowl hunting in the United States since 1991. In Canada, recommendations to require powderless shells are in the works.

Lead shot can be used for hunting upland birds and, if lightly loaded, on neighborhood kids stealing your watermelons. The most widely used nontoxic shot for ducks and geese is made of steel, and the use of that metal has been roundly endorsed by the American Dental Cap Association. Other metals used in more powerful nontoxic shot include bismuth and combinations of tungsten-iron, tungsten-polymer, and tungsten-nickel-iron, and these combinations knock the snot out of ducks and geese at a longer range than steel shot. Successful lobbying by the National Scrap Metal Coalition and New Age Dump has recently approved new combinations: tungsten-bismuth-iron, iron-bismuth-tungsten, bismuth-iron-tungsten, tungsten-iron-bismuth, iron-tungsten-bismuth, bismuth-tungsten-iron, or any other combination of the three. The costs associated with developing, manufacturing, and marketing these nontoxic shells can induce toxic sticker shock at the retail counter.

SAFETY EQUIPMENT

Having hunted in target-rich environments with nonresidents and other village idiots, Buck recommends the following minimum safety equipment.

EYES

Your eyes are your most precious possession in your head, so wear shooting glasses made from shatterproof polycarbonate; wear a wraparound version if hunting with politicians. If the politicians have had a beer lunch, the Birdshot

Safety Council highly recommends a reinforced football helmet with a polycarbonate face shield, along with "double-tin" clothing—made from paraffin-treated, heavy-duty cotton duck cloth—from the neck down.

Shooting conditions vary widely, so purchase glasses frames with interchangeable lenses, including polarized lenses for shooting ducks that dive below the water surface.

EARS

Sound is measured in units of decibel (dB)—or, in Canada, percent of blood alcohol content. Human perception of sound, as measured in decibels, runs from 0 dB to more than 175 dB, the latter equivalent to the sound level of your mother-in-law on the toilet. Most firearm noise hovers around the 150-dB level, unless you are in your truck with your firestick poked out the window. Noise levels at your spouse's family reunions approach supersonic levels; constant exposure can cripple your success at the office and in the sporting fields.

If you are hunting birds with good friends or listening to your teenagers or your spouse, simple ear protection such as cotton balls, a pencil eraser, or a foam plug is satisfactory. If you prefer to use chewing gum, the Double Bubble brand is recommended by most ear-canal surgeons. And it can be rechewed after use in foreign countries such as Arkansas and Mississippi.

More expensive in-the-canal earplugs have applications out of the field as well; they are especially handy in the lodge, after the shoot, when the truth squad has left for the day. Target-rich environments require more serious protection: over-the-ear "muffs" or special inner-canal electronic units filter out loud sounds and enhance low-frequency noises, which can be very handy if an office is in the grip of a hostile takeover.

BIRD DECOYS

Both migratory birds on their way cross-country to breed and nest, and those just flying across a field for food and water, are attracted to real or imagined brethren on the ground or water. Waterfowl are the easiest to fool, but there is no agreement, especially among hunting guides, about which type of decoy to use, much less where. Decoy types, however, are many.

DUCK AND GEESE DECOYS

FULL-BODY DECOYS: These are three-dimensional ducks and geese, life-sized, supersized, and super-duper-sized in various postures. Most are made from a heavy, high-tech plastic. Some hunters use taxidermy geese for greater effect. Others use plastic miniatures or motion decoys; by the time the bird gets close enough to understand the deception, a crash landing follows. Note that motorized decoys are prohibited in states that don't listen to Rush Limbaugh.

> **BUCK'S BONUS TIP: Nonresidents and your in-laws will shoot your decoys sometime during the season. Do not set your antique blow-up decoys within their range. Foam-filled decoys are your only option.**

HALF-BODY DECOY: Half-ducks have a comic aspect. Puddle-duck butts pointed skyward in the water indicate either good grub or adolescent ducks mooning airborne elders.

BUCK'S BONUS TIP: **Piles of goose-turd decoys are most effective for attracting park and golf-course geese. Buck's decoy company, Willapa Bay Ca-Ca Ltd., offers standard- and magnum-sized turds with proprietary interlocking technology. Biodegradable and safe for little children to eat, the realistic-looking packing-peanut-sized poop is green and white and embedded with small, crushed feathers.**

SHELL DECOY: Closest to a full body in two dimensions, a shell decoy is stackable. Magnum honker-goose shells serve two purposes: attracting magnum honkers, and, with the largest, as a blind. For the latter use, stick the shotgun muzzle out the rear of the decoy. The smoky noise will be familiar to any goose following too close in V formation.

SILHOUETTE DECOY: These are flat cutouts with digitally enhanced, textured photographic images on them. They are attached to sticks that are hard to pound into frozen ground. Geese flying directly over these decoys think their relatives below are bulimic.

WIND SOCK DECOY: Similar to a runway air sock, these decoys twist in the wind, anchored at the "breast" opening with a head on a stick. Game birds appreciate knowing the wind conditions on landing strips, especially since those in the control tower are armed.

RAG DECOY: Large displays to attract snow geese can be costly without the use of white rags. Rag decoys can be as simple as pieces of white bed sheets—or bar napkins—laid on the ground. Your wife's bloomers can also be used as wind sock or rag decoys. Use only her clean underpants; otherwise, you'll never keep the dogs in the blind. If your wife has a big heinie, her garments can be used to decoy geese too. Your mother-in-law's extra-extra-extra-large panties are recommended for speckled geese.

> **BUCK'S BONUS TIP:** Ducks that normally feed in cornfields will land where corn on the cob is still available. You can't put corn out—that would be illegal "baiting"—but what's to stop you from painting your empty beer cans yellow and throwing them around your blind? When the ducks drop in for a "brewski," show them that happy hour has ended.

CONFIDENCE DECOYS

Confidence decoys signal safety to migrating birds in flight, and there are several types available:

FULL-SIZED WATERFOWL IMITATIONS

If migrating birds see all decoys with a heads-up position, they may sense danger—or, more likely, they may not have any thoughts at all in their bony little heads. Overly cautious waterfowlers mix "sleeper" and "feeder" decoys in the spread. Sleeper decoys have the head tucked into its back feathers, as if preening, and feeders have corn falling from their bills.

NOTE: If you put only sleepers out, the flight may think its nighttime and fall asleep in the air, to predictable, disastrous results. Feeder decoys are most common with geese field spreads, other than "pooping" goose decoys. Additional decoy goose heads are available: feeder heads that feed right or left, resters with one eye open (left or right), geese with a squinted eye taking a dump, and high-necked lookouts.

BUCK'S BONUS TIP: No matter which decoys you use, place an uneven number of decoys in the spread. An unpaired single attracts horny drake mallards.

THE ULTIMATE MALLARD DUCK CONFIDENCE DECOY

 TIP ADDENDUM: The use of an uneven number of decoys is an old wives' tale and waterfowlers, in particular, prefer younger wives.

 WARNING: Nonresident hunters build confidence by shooting resident hunters' decoys while the locals are packing it in.

FULL-SIZED NON-DUCK/GOOSE IMITATIONS

Waterfowl seem to understand that the presence of a normally nervous great blue heron and/or egret signals a safe landing zone. These wary marsh birds do not tame easily without drugs. And they would rather just be left alone, to the dismay of waterfront developers promising huggable nature. A single blue heron or egret also attracts very curious, horny drake mallards.

BLINDS

A blind is any construction—natural or man-made—that hunters use to hide from the view of the hunted. A game bird won't know the occupants of the blind are blind until they start shooting.

WHEN TO USE A BLIND

UPLAND-BIRD HUNTING: Since upland-bird hunting is done mostly in motion, there is little need for formal blinds. Even turkey hunters need only a tree to sit against. And all bird hunters would agree that there is certainly no need for blinds on the bedroom window of that young housewife across the cul-de-sac.

WATERFOWL HUNTING: Migrating birds present two distinct shooting opportunities: pass shooting and decoy shooting. The challenge is to turn the former into the latter by encouraging passing birds to cluster near decoys. This maneuver calls for you to hide as best you can. Substantial money can be saved by investing in blinds rather than the latest camouflage clothing.

RECOMMENDED BLINDS

GENERAL: If available, use natural objects that birds are used to seeing, such as an old tractor, a rock pile, an abandoned Ford 150 pickup, a farm animal silhouette (see "Confidence Decoys," page 27), or (for your brother-in-law) a manure pile.

EARLY SEASON: Immature, trusting birds arrive early. Tactics vary from hiding—say, in heavy cover, in standing corn, or in a brushy ditch or fence line—or building a blind with natural materials and/or a metal frame with camouflage cloth.

BUCK'S BONUS TIP: Never underestimate the power of manure on and in your brother-in-law's blind. Shiny man-made materials and human faces flare birds.

LATE SEASON: Late-season birds are wary, so blinds must be refreshed with more brush and manure. When ducks and geese start to feed in the middle of an open field, just out of range, pop-up blinds are used by guides who are too lazy to dig pits in the frozen ground. Tip them less.

BUCK'S BONUS TIP: Move the pop-up close to your in-law so you can poke him with a stick when the birds arrive.

LATE SEASON IN SNOW COUNTRY: A Christmas goose can be had while hiding under a white bedsheet—at home in the bedroom, and in the field.

A proven alternative in frozen, snow-covered eastern Washington in late December is a Styrofoam "camp" box built for hunter occupancy.

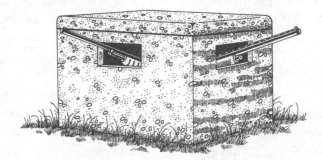

GEESE TRICKED BY THIS BLIND MANEUVER NEVER TRUST CAMPERS AGAIN

BLIND FENG SHUI

The use of feng (wind) shui (water) guidelines in building a duck-hunting blind assure a harmonious balance of yin and yang and a refreshed alignment with Uranus.

- ✔ The entrance door should have a clear line of sight, especially to the dog that ate last night's venison chili.

- ✔ Wind chimes and crystals shift energy in a space, and their use will shift major energy into your personal space.

- ✔ Pools of flowing water in the blind will direct major exit energy into open space.

- ✔ Windows should be positioned to allow for a flow of air, purifying a climate poisoned by a retriever that ate last night's venison chili.

LATE SEASON IN THE DAKOTAS AND NORTHERN MINNESOTA: The best blind in subzero, inhuman temperatures is a toasty SUV outfitted with studs or chains, cruising the back roads, looking for birds in likely hidey-holes, ready to launch "shock and awe" ambushes.

P.S.: Ask your cable company to add *Buck's This Old Duck Shack*, a groundbreaking program bursting with tips on how to remodel your primary residence.

BIRD DOGS

There is scant literature on hunting dogs, and it's the author's hope that someday we'll be able to read expert opinions on which breed is best for which bird species and habitats. It certainly would be good to learn the differences between pointers and retrievers. It is further hoped that we could receive that advice on television, perhaps on a channel devoted to outdoor activities or on video or DVD. Until that information is readily available, Buck would like to offer his observations from his seminal work in dog breeding, training, and fieldwork. Buck's kennels are located at the lodge next to his Advanced Plucking Institute; since the discovery of large applicators of pepper spray, they are less often sublet to the sheriff at the close of happy hour in the Vallhaha Lounge.

GENERAL OBSERVATIONS

✔ For a bird hunter, dogs are like people, only better.

✔ Never feed string to a dog unless a butt-scoot across your carpet is your idea of home decorating.

✔ Any three-legged field dog has a leg up on any show dog.

HUNTING EQUIPMENT

✔ Large labs are great for crashing wild pheasants out of standing corn.

✔ Trust the work ethic of any dog named Dog or addressed by its coat color, such as Brownie, Blackie, or Whitey.

✔ A work ethic will be absent in any dog with a blue-blood name such as Chip, Tiffany, or Reggie, or addressed by its owner's surname such as Baron von Fartsack IIIXV.

✔ A trained Chesapeake Bay retriever is a "shock and awe" force to be reckoned with.

✔ It's not a good sign if the guide's dog takes a leak on your leg.

✔ All dogs enjoy a roll on a fresh cow pie or a rotting salmon carcass.

✔ You can lean on any dog that leans against you.

✔ The reason dogs lick their nuts is that they know you can't.

BUCK'S LARGE BONUS TIP: If you ever find yourself in a crowd of beribboned field-champion owners, don't try to stake out territory among that preening bluster. These individuals command the known world of obscure bloodlines, so create a world of your own. Start with, "Do you know what kind of hunting dog Catherine the Great used?" Mention your dog's fondness for beets, boiled cabbage, and vodka chasers. While the befuddled gentry scratch their coifs and their blue bloods lick each other's nuts, buy a round of drinks for the show-dog widows at the other end of the bar. There'll be a few "breeders" in that neglected bunch.

BUCK'S MEDIUM BONUS TIP: Use a silent dog whistle to enhance the chaos of championship field trials.

 BUCK'S SMALL BONUS TIP: In the field, if the championship retriever is behaving badly and the owner is not looking, slip the critter a strong laxative placed inside some ground meat.

If just the championship *owner* is behaving badly (and not looking), scratch the dog on all the parts it can't normally reach, put a dead bird in the dog's mouth, and start pulling on the bird as if you're playing a game. Then show the dog where you last saw the skunk.

UPDATE ON BREEDING MULTITASKING HYBRIDS

In the waterfowl category, if you cross a male labrador retriever with a female poodle, you get a labradoodle. If you cross a male Chesapeake Bay retriever with a female chihuahua, you get a very sore chihuahua. In the upland category, if you cross an English springer spaniel with a labrador, you get a labradinger—on rare occasions, a giant labrahumdinger. But if you cross a brussels griffon with a brussels sprout, you'll still end up with a vegetable.

MORE BUCK'S BONUS TIPS

✔ When picking your seat in a duck blind, locate where the retriever usually enters, then sit at the opposite end of the blind. By the time the lab reaches you for a nut scratch, its coat will be dry.

✔ In a really cold goose pit, ask before putting your hands in the hunting guide's warm pants pockets.

HUNTING EQUIPMENT

✔ Ducks in the wild live from one to seven years on average. So an old duck's life is equal to half a dog's life—and, in human terms, one-seventh of a Norwegian bachelor farmer's life. Wild ducks avoid Buck's lodge in northern Minnesota and hide out in Wisconsin, where they can live for up to twenty years.

✔ A classic decoy spread is the pipe pattern. In the Midwest, the corncob pattern has passed its heyday. In states that vote Democrat, a nonsmoking pattern prevails.

✔ South Dakota is due south of North Dakota. The way to distinguish between the two is to note that South Dakota has one more tree. After the first winter whiteout, however, it's hard to tell the difference until spring, which arrives in the middle of the following year.

✔ Nonresidents make the mistake of setting drake decoys facing hen decoys. This position is not found in nature, especially late in the season, when drakes are mighty tired of hearing that incessant migratory nag-quacking. Face drake decoys in the opposite direction.

✔ Scouting where migrating waterfowl feed is critical to hunting success. Residents can be hired as scouts, but Indians near Custer, South Dakota, are unlikely prospects.

✔ In the general population, right-handed shooters rule, by roughly 85 percent to 14 percent. One percent of shooters lost a hand in a farm accident. Right-handed shooters shoot best going from right to left, while the reverse is true for southpaws. Above the equator, more ducks move from right to left, so right-handed shooters do best, especially in North Dakota, where a complete circle can be made without hitting a tree. Below the equator, left-handed shooters, especially those who are left-eye dominant and roaming, end up with more señoritas down at the topless—er, tapas bar.

HUNTING TECHNIQUES: GENERAL

Those with the highest test scores at the end of this primer will be awarded an honorary membership in the National Boom and Crock-Pot Society, Northernmost Minnesota Chapter, and a lap dance by one of Buck's first wives.

MASTER EYE

One eye dominates your aiming ability. Your "master" eye normally corresponds to whether you are right- or left-handed. Buck, a major shooter, is a special case: his left eye is dominant, but he uses his right hand during lap dances at the club.

The quickest test to determine your master eye is to flip the bird at the boss or his office kingdom with both eyes open. Now close one eye, and you'll see which eye now focuses on his call to Human Resources.

The following are four typical master-eye scenarios:

RIGHT-EYE DOMINANT

If you are right-handed, aiming is easy and automatic, especially if you shot your left eye out in a childhood BB-gun accident, despite Mom's warnings to be careful. If you are left-handed, it will appear that you are leading the bird enough.

LEFT-EYE DOMINANT

If you are right-handed, you'll need to shoot left-handed; with most autoloaders, you will also experience ejection debris. If you lost your right hand in a farm accident, you'll park in the handicapped zone at the public-access area anyway.

HUNTING TECHNIQUES: GENERAL

THE TEN COMMANDMENTS OF FIREARM SAFETY

1. ALWAYS POINT THE MUZZLE IN A SAFE DIRECTION—OR AT SOMETHING YOU WANT TO SHOOT THAT IS GOOD ON THE BARBECUE.

2. NEVER POACH A GAME BIRD OUT OF SEASON—OR WITHOUT SEASONINGS.

3. KEEP YOUR FINGER OFF THE TRIGGER UNTIL YOU ARE READY TO SHOOT. IF YOUR SHOTGUN HAS A DOUBLE TRIGGER, KEEP BOTH FINGERS OFF THE TRIGGERS.

4. IF YOU AND YOUR WIFE ARE HAVING MARITAL DIFFICULTIES, KEEP YOUR FIREARMS LOCKED IN A SECURE PLACE AND STORE THE AMMUNITION IN YOUR TRUNK.

5. TREAT EVERY FIREARM CARRIED BY AN IN-LAW AS IF IT WERE LOADED WITH ITS SAFETY OFF.

6. DON'T SLEEP WITH YOUR LOADED SHOTGUN UNLESS YOUR IN-LAWS ARE SHARING YOUR ROOM.

7. DO NOT SHOOT A DEER-CROSSING SIGN WITH A SHOTGUN EXCEPT DURING SLUG SEASON.

8. NEVER SHOOT ACROSS A ROADWAY—UNLESS IT'S A CHICKEN CROSSING THE ROAD JUST TO PROVE THAT IT CAN.

9. IF YOU HUNT BIRDS ON A HORSE, COVER THE ANIMAL'S EARS BEFORE FIRING.

10. AT THE FIRING RANGE, DO NOT TELL THE RANGE OFFICERS THAT MARINES ARE NAVY MP'S.

CROSSED-EYE DOMINANT

If the focal point of your cross is at the barrel tip, your field of fire will expand with distance. If the focal point is thirty to forty yards away, your aim should be dead-on.

CROSS-DRESSED DOMINANT

See "Sporting Clays," page 47.

TRAP SHOOTING

If judged by the typical upland-bird game bag, practice does not make perfect. Any bird shooter can, however, lose good form during the off-season. A simple preseason practice is to dry-mount your shotgun in the privacy of your home.

> **BUCK'S BONUS TIP:** It doesn't hurt to let her mother see your serious focus on being a good provider—and lord and master. It will encourage the old bat to support your "elsewhere" shooting games such as trap, skeet, and sporting clays.

One of the original two forms of competitive shotgun shooting, trap shooting differs from skeet shooting in that there is only one "house" that throws targets, and the shooters only move through five positions.

Originally, the targets were live birds, including the then-abundant passenger pigeon. Once these were thinned out, fake birds replaced the more edible ones. Glass balls stuffed with feathers were once popular and are now collector's items. Eventually, they were replaced by the clay pigeon, a small, flat disk made from nontoxic, biodegradable clay. Disks are painted fluorescent orange for better visibility, and to resemble the fluorescent orange game birds found near nuclear-contaminated Superfund sites. Clay pigeons are thrown into the air or rolled along the ground to resemble running, wounded birds; rabbits; and yappy little neighborhood dogs that need to be taught a lesson.

HISTORICAL NOTE: The effort to replace trap passenger pigeons with bald eagles was halted when the national emblem was recruited for parcel post.

Trap shooting has its own rules, equipment, and etiquette.

TYPES OF TRAP SHOOTING

OLYMPIC TRAP SHOOTING: Olympic trap shooting is the most familiar international version. The fifteen Olympic fixed-angle machines ensure equal difficulty for all. Men fire 125 rounds each; women 75 rounds. The village idiots of the host country collect the shell casings for firewood. There is a twenty-five-shot finale for the top six competitors. Olympic clay targets fly at seventy-five miles per hour (or thirty-seven hectares, Canadian), which means Olympic champions are best suited in the field for shooting low-flying aircraft, UFOs, and teal flying in gale-force winds. A variation on Olympic is double trap, where two identical targets are thrown simultaneously; since so few are identical, this event is rarely staged. An even less familiar version is the Nordic trap, in which competitors are required to eat a pound of lutefisk or an English pot pie one hour before the event and rotate through the five shooting stations before being allowed to use an Olympic-sized restroom.

AMERICAN TRAP SHOOTING: American trap has three categories: sixteen-yard singles, sixteen-yard doubles, and handicap, at distances between nineteen and twenty-seven yards. In singles, the shooter takes one shot at each of five targets, in each of the five positions, sixteen yards behind the trap house. In doubles, two targets are thrown at the same time, and the shooter is allowed one shot per target. There is no second shot at any target in singles or in handicap. Handicap is played the same way as singles, but from a longer distance. You start at twenty yards from the target and earn yardage back if you shoot a score of at least ninety-six (or sleep with the range master). Ladies and juniors start at nineteen yards. Lap dancers from the local gentlemen's clubs start pretty much wherever they want to, usually from the range master's Winnebago.

In most states, there is no requirement to be handicapped to shoot handicap; however, in states along our northern border, adult Canadians fall into the handicapped category. In handicap, each participant in a squad of five shoots twenty-five shells at twenty-five clay pigeons. In corporate American trap shooting, most favored by Republican executives, stool pigeons are the preferred targets.

TRAP-SHOOTING EQUIPMENT

Most trap is shot with 12-gauge shotguns. Some prefer a 20 gauge, and double-barreled shotguns are becoming more popular than single barrels. Lead shotshells in sizes between 7 and 9, with a dram-equivalent rating of 3, is preferred. Special competition trap-shooting shotguns have finger grooves in the forearm area, adjustable straight combs, and adjustable recoil-reduction systems. There is much hilarity when these specialty guns are brought into Buck's duck blind.

TRAP-SHOOTING ETIQUETTE

Good manners prevail on the best trap courses, since unusual behavior can affect the performance of other squad members. If your squad is seriously behind in the competition, however, unusual behavior should become a squad imperative. Loud, vulgar language has a place in such circumstances, as do air horns, steel drums, and replicas of Civil War cannons.

Individual movement is between positions or stations, and is right to left. An exception is made when the shooters are all either left-handed, left-eye dominant but using right-handed shotguns, or a mixture of the two. Left-eye-dominant right-handers—"temporary southpaws"—who are shooting semiautomatics with right-hand ejection can be recognized easily in the club by their facial powder burns. Shotguns must be open when moving between stations, unless a flock of teal are in range or a nearby company squad needs help.

In the beginning, the shooter at position number one shoots first by calling, "Pull!" to the puller or scorer. Nonmembers are required to say, "Please pull," until they can outshoot the inebriated members. Once each shooter has completed a round, the scorer will call out, "Change positions."

> **BUCK'S BONUS TIP:** Tip the scorer in advance of the competition for special scoring considerations. Normally, the scorer will call out, "Hit!" or "Miss!" on each shot. A sympathetic scorer will use such phrases as "near miss" and "holy smoke, you really nailed that one."

In Arkansas, Alabama, and Mississippi, a paying guest can shoot the trap house that throws a broken clay pigeon. In Canada, only residents of the host province can shoot the responsible range master, but it must be with a shotgun that is registered with a local brewery official.

SKEET SHOOTING

Skeet shooting is acknowledged to have been founded by an avid grouse hunter in 1915 and is meant to simulate the field action of bird hunting. As with trap shooting, live birds were the original targets, and the original rules of engagement included a ban on shooting the birds while they were still in the cage—unless they couldn't be hit in the air.

Skeet shooting differs from trap shooting primarily with the use of two trap houses—a "high" and a "low"—and three additional positions.

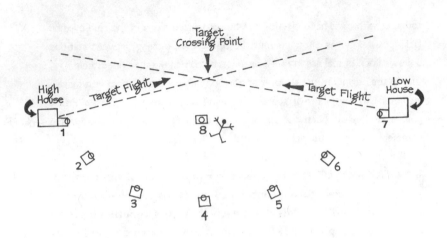

TYPES OF SKEET SHOOTING

OLYMPIC SKEET SHOOTING: Skeet shooting has had official Olympic status since 1896, with women allowed to compete with men in 1968. Yet in 1993, women were no longer allowed to compete with men. However, once women shooters around the world learned of this arbitrary decision and told their husband-judges that they just shot their last "wad," a woman's skeet event reappeared in the Olympic program.

In Olympic skeet shooting, there is a zero- to three-second delay after the shooter has called for the targets. This delay is difficult for older male shooters, who forget during the delay when or why they asked for a target. Older female shooters going through a difficult divorce or menopause suffer penalties for "jumping the gun," so to speak, by firing at the targets before they leave the trap house—or, in worse divorce-case scenarios, at a range master.

AMERICAN SKEET SHOOTING: American skeet shooting does allow the shooter to call for the target with the gun on the shoulder, and to shoot at targets without delay. The action is more complicated than trap shooting, to wit:

A skeet shooter shoots from seven positions on a semicircle and an eighth position halfway between stations one and seven. The trap houses sit at each corner of the semicircle. At stations one and two, single targets are launched from the high house first, and then from the low house, and then two targets are launched simultaneously. At stations three, four, and five, single targets are launched from the high house first, then the low—or is it from the low then the high house? At stations six and seven, single targets are launched again from the high house first, and then the low, and then a double target is launched. At station eight, one high and one low target are launched. A shooter must shoot his first missed target, and if no targets are missed, the shooter must shoot the twenty-fifth shell at low station eight before the train leaves for all points north of Grand Central Station.

There are other national versions of skeet shooting that have no international recognition and are designed to let lesser shooters succeed. For example, English skeet allows scullery maids to stand in for the financially and morally bankrupt masters of the manse.

SKEET-SHOOTING EQUIPMENT

Skeet shooters have a wider range of permissible firearms to use: 12-gauge shotguns, and the small gauges: 20, 28, and .410. As in trap shooting, skeet shooters are required or advised to wear eye and ear protection. For hearing, this insurance can be as simple as small tubular foam plugs or a fresh wad of Double Bubble bubble gum. Serious shooters, however, opt for hearing protection that covers the ear or protects the ear canal with sophisticated noise-blocking *and* amplifying technology. This latest equipment allows the shooter to hear previously unheard conversations (such as what the scorers and bleacher-seat denizens are saying about you and your family lineage) and blocking noises that are unpleasant (mother-in-law) or harmful (shotgun blasts).

> **BUCK'S BONUS TIP:** When retiring an older-model ear-canal noise blocker, consider the needs of your faithful canine hunting companion. Old Blue would also appreciate not hearing from her side of the family again!

SKEET-SHOOTING ETIQUETTE

Scorers are only human. If you sense they are missing some of your better shots, shout, "Got it!" after hits that are in question. "Nailed that one!" is an acceptable substitute. As is, "Holy shit, did you see that shot?" It's not uncommon for scorers to favor local hitters. So, unless you tip them properly before the competition, they have little or no understanding of your commitment to do well.

Tipping a local scoring official is a gracious act if performed properly. Scorers certainly don't expect unsolicited gifts, so don't be surprised by their surprise. Here are several guidelines: Approach the scorer in a semiprivate or private area—like a washroom (also called a men's room, or a "shitter" in Connecticut). Present the gratuity in an unmarked envelope, personalized with their name. The gratuity should be in the form of negotiable paper with presidents' images on them, or bonds and stocks. Coins are not recommended, nor are gift cards for restaurants where food orders are barked from the car window into a clown's face. If there are any difficulties in the washroom, where the scorer just doesn't understand the importance of your gracious act, quickly repocket the envelope, pull your pants and shorts down, and hobble out of the area, calling for range security.

> **BUCK'S SHOOTING TIP:** A tall shooter has no advantage hitting targets coming from the high house. The corollary is also true; short shooters are not more successful on birds out of the short house. It should be mentioned, though, that in general, tall people are more successful than short people—especially those who play basketball well.

SPORTING CLAYS

Sporting clays differs from trap and skeet shooting in that the clay pigeons are intended to imitate the flight habits of different game birds, and occasionally rabbits, in natural habitats. It's not clear where bird hunters find flying rabbits, but they are more likely to do so after a liquid lunch.

The British origin of sporting clays ensures as loose an organizational structure as golf at St. Andrews, yet noisier—except at the latter's nineteenth hole. The shooting area typically consists of five to ten stations ("butts" in England), where pairs of clay pigeons are thrown in ways that represent the aforementioned animals. Three types of pairs are thrown: (1) report pairs, in which the second pigeon is thrown when the first shot is taken; (2) following pairs, in which one is thrown right after another; and (3) simultaneous pairs, in which both pigeons are thrown at the same time. Sporting clays is optimal for expensive double-barreled shotguns. At Buck's Lodge in northern Minnesota, ten to twenty clay pigeons are thrown at once, so those shooting automatics with the plugs out will have optimum flock-shooting.

THE QUARRY

In addition to the standard clay bird used in trap and skeet shooting, sporting-clay targets include mini, midi, battue, rocket, and rabbit "pigeons."

STANDARD CLAY TARGET: A flat disk four and one-quarter inches across and about one inch in height; there is nothing comparable in nature, unless you include medium-sized, sun-baked cow pies.

MIDI CLAY TARGET: A smaller, thinner, calf-sized cowpie.

MINI CLAY TARGET: An even smaller, thinner disk, comparable to a small, flattened fauna.

BATTUE CLAY TARGET: A very thin disk, comparable to oversized crackers at a club cocktail reception, or your first-communion wafer but without the cheap wine.

ROCKET CLAY TARGET: With the same diameter as the standard and about half the height, this disk will drive even the best shooters to drink—which accounts for much of their behavior at home too.

RABBIT CLAY TARGET: A ground-bouncing disk that prepares you for ground-sluicing game birds.

EQUIPMENT

✔ A fine double-barreled 12-gauge shotgun and ever-so-lightly loaded shotshells.

✔ Ear protection, such as inner-ear devices or earmuffs, that provide noise reduction not only from the rounds fired but also from judges mocking your gear or shooting.

✔ Polycarbonate shooting glasses, in defense of flying objects.

RULES OF PLAY

✔ A shooter may be inspected for proper, tidy sporting clay clothing and assorted gentlemen's leather goods.

✔ A shooter may start with a low- or premounted gun when the target is called whatever a target is called that day.

✔ Only two shells—and no contest participants—may be loaded.

✔ Avoid accidental discharge, and humor club elders who do.

HUNTING TECHNIQUES: GENERAL

✔ If doubles (a pair thrown at the same or almost the same time) are tossed and both are broken, the two are counted as kills. They are also considered to be a major miracle, as recorded by the local diocese.

✔ A malfunction of the gun is counted as a lost bird. It is also another reason to throw you off the clubhouse grounds.

✔ Scoring is the responsibility of a field judge who seems to live beyond his or her years. Scoring is recorded as hit, miss, lost, or dead. Hit and dead are similar; the latter is used when the clay pigeon stops breathing. Missed is marked unless the judge's opinion is placed in dispute; in that case, spectators are allowed one second opinion and one throwing tomato per person. Scores tallied in pencil leave room for financial considerations at the end of the competition (see Buck's Bonus Tip, page 43).

✔ If the day is really looking to go sideways, amp it up by engraving your name or initials on the fancy over-under of the membership chairman who turned your application down—when no one is looking—and report the theft.

✔ The most X's in the hit boxes win the match—and a chance to win a ride in the club manager's Buick.

BUCK'S BONUS TIP: The irrelevance of sporting clays to field action is in its scoring. A clay pigeon with a small, visible chip counts as much as one that is completely smashed. So if you are practicing for a late-season sea-duck hunt, shoot the clay pigeon hard and often: as it exits the thrower, while in flight, and on the ground, until it stops moving. Please note that this deviation from clubhouse rules might trigger censure.

PATTERNING

The most important preseason exercise is measuring pellet "spread," also known as patterning. The easiest way is to take your firestick out back and fire at targets fixed distances away. Only then will you know your odds of wiping the smile off a game bird.

If, for example, you normally shoot decoying ducks from thirty yards away, place a target at that distance and fire several rounds to determine pattern. In a housing development's cul-de-sac, you won't be able to factor in wind resistance, but you can count on a few calls to 911. There are charts that measure all the variables, but most hunting guides will not hold those charts (or targets) for you while you shoot.

Any target will do. Tack some paper on a fence, preferably the neighbor's fence, making sure the little lady next door isn't hanging out her wash behind the fence. Draw a big circle and, for more focused shooting, add a duck or chukar or your boss's face or butt in the center. Measure your normal shooting distance for upland birds or waterfowl, and fire into the target using a variety of shotgun loads through a variety of chokes. A shotgun with a full choke should have the highest concentration of pellets inside the circle. A brother-in-law's shotgun will produce the lowest concentration, as you can see.

HUNTING TECHNIQUES: GENERAL

WIND AS A SHOOTING VARIABLE

Game birds cruise at varying speeds, which are influenced by the bird's body shape and weight, and by weather conditions. Fat, domesticated, urban birds obey posted speed limits, but wild, rural birds fly with reckless abandon.

Wild mallards fly at speeds up to fifty-five miles per hour; pheasants fly a little slower, especially one with an eighty-pound lab hanging on to its tail. Hens fly a little slower, which makes them better targets for nonresidents and other developmentally disabled individuals.

Many of the smaller eastern upland birds—quail, grouse, robins, and woodcock—fly much slower, so there is no excuse for an empty game bag for upland bird-hunting crybabies. There are, however, very good excuses for an empty bag when hunting western chukar (see "Reasons to Give Up," page 2007).

In the rare event there is no wind, hunters should lead a duck about ten feet within average shooting range. Upland bird hunters need less lead distance when shooting birds on the ground. Birds flying into the wind are slowed by the air currents, and your shot pattern will be pushed into the same current, so continue to lead the bird. Birds flying with the wind will arrive at the feeding grounds before their scheduled serving time, so shoot them first, if you can see them.

The flight of game birds is also subject to field alterations in their body shape.

NORMAL FLIGHT SPEEDS PREVAIL WITH A HEALTHY, HAPPY GAME BIRD

FLIGHT WITH ONE WING DAMAGED OR MISSING MAKES THE BIRD CIRCLE MORE; THE DAMAGED WING DOESN'T SLOW THE BIRD DOWN

FLIGHT WITH A DAMAGED COCKPIT SLOWS CONSIDERABLY WHEN THE VIEW AHEAD IS OBSTRUCTED OR MISSING

SHOOTING ETIQUETTE

Etiquette is a code word for crowd control. When a crowd is armed, generally agreed-upon codes of conduct reduce the need for emergency medical services.

UPLAND-BIRD HUNTING

Lodge manners extend into the field as members chase upland birds. Club members' age, physical condition, and personal history rule. The more senior shooters take the first shot out of their estate wagons; the infirm shoot next; they are followed by those with minority club ownership. Shooters walking the field decide on individual fields of fire, making sure at least one attorney is in the crossfire. In approaching a championship pointing dog, one person readies to shoot, while the other kicks the dog in the nuts. When hunting alone, all rules become null and void, but caution is advised if you notice the lens flash from the warden's spotting scope.

WATERFOWL HUNTING

Hunting guides assign fields of fire in a blind based on presumed end-of-hunt tipping (see "Guide to Tipping," page 171). Left-hand shooters shoot left, right-hand shooters shoot right, and ambidextrous shooters take head-on and periphery shots that irritate everyone. Those using double-barreled shotguns are encouraged to stay at the lodge. Waterfowl can be shot down from a powerboat, with the engine off. Shooters positioned in the bow who abruptly stand to shoot will have an opportunity to retrieve their own birds.

SUMMARY OF GOVERNMENT HUNTING REGULATIONS

STATE REGULATIONS

On opening day of bird-hunting season, no one may possess more birds than is allowed under the daily bag limit. The one exception is when the armed individual holding the bag appears to be possessed, according to modern psychological criteria or the doctrine of the Mother Church.

Hunters must make a reasonable effort to retrieve dead or crippled birds, even if they have to wait until the farmer with the shotgun leaves his front porch and goes to bed.

Upland birds may be shot down from a motorized vehicle if that vehicle has come to a complete stop, either by accident or by running out of gas, with one exception: upland geese may be shot from a moving golf cart. Plantation birds may be taken down from the horse-drawn carriage if the horse or the horse driver is hard of hearing.

> **BUCK'S BONUS TIP:** Unwritten Mississippi, Alabama, Arkansas regulation: Yankees must be watched at all times, especially around our womenfolk.

When retrieving decoys, hunters may encounter crab pots. In most areas, tourist boards allow the emptying of one crab pot a day, as long as no other boats are in view.

All duck boats must carry one U.S. Coast Guard (USCG)–approved wearable personal flotation device life preserver, or one large woman or man (two hundred pounds or more), for each person in the boat. Boats longer than sixteen feet must carry at least one USCG-approved type six throwable flotation device. Grappling hooks are *not* USCG approved, and beer coolers are no longer acceptable as primary life-saving devices in the water. Beer coolers are recognizable life-saving devices on land, however.

During open waterfowl season, hunters may not leave a boat untended unless they have to go number one or number two. If they have to go both number one *and* number two, a mother-in-law packed the lunch.

Any blind on public property is considered public property unless the armed individual who built the blind is in residence at the time.

No person may hunt migratory waterfowl using a sink box. A sink box is a structure that allows a hunter to hide beneath the water surface. In contrast, a stink box is a structure shared by an in-law, and there should be a law against that too.

Hunters may not string decoys across public access to waterways, unless they don't want others to hunt there.

FEDERAL REGULATIONS

Every hunter should consult the Code of Federal Regulations, Title 50, Part 20, Section 14–240, Code of Conduct for Camouflaged Individuals Not in Military Service, except where superceded by and subject to Homeland Security Regulation 69, Table/Lap Dance Expense Allowance for Federal Employees.

SUMMATION

You may not hunt with, from, using, while, or by_____.
[To be completed by warden.]

OTHER REGULATIONS

LICENSES: Unless you are on your own property, cannot be seen from the road, are surrounded by good, trustworthy neighbors, and are out of earshot of wardens with parabolic listening devices, you may need a bird-hunting license—except in states that begin with the letter A, and the east side of New York City. License costs vary, most notably by state resident and non-resident status. To be safe, multiply the cost of a resident license by five to estimate the cost of a nonresident license. A portion of the nonresident license revenue goes to the local chapter of the Audubon Society for game-bird hospital bills.

Typical required licenses include the following:

✔ A small-game license, unless you plan to shoot large geese.

✔ A valid state upland-bird/waterfowl stamp, along with your signature across your face.

✔ A valid unstamped federal migratory bird-hunting conservation stamp.

✔ A notarized letter of permission to shoot geese from your neighbor's dock.

✔ A hunter-safety certificate or diploma from the American Anger Management Institute (proof of firearm-safety training should include the attending emergency-room physician's notes).

✔ A ticket to the warden's ball.

✔ A note from a Bureau of Alcohol, Tobacco, and Firearms agent stating that you are old enough to buy cigarettes.

✔ A birth certificate stating that you were born on or before the Year of the Peking Duck, A.D.

Military personnel on leave may hunt without a permit, but those serving in armored divisions are not permitted to use large-bore firearms borrowed from the local guard unit.

ACCIDENTAL HARVEST WITHOUT A LICENSE: On the rare occasions when he drives really fast at the right time of day, a sportsman might accidentally "take" a game bird with a motorized vehicle or boat. These events fall outside the norm, yet it is best to prepare for such an event.

A pheasant taken by a pickup on a dusty farm road delineating cornfields should be considered a gift, as should a drake mallard taken by a bass boat gone astray. Caution is advised, however: this technique is used by the game wardens who can't catch off-road hunters to fill their own freezer. But if the warden's own grillwork is full of feathers, they've done well enough not to worry about a sportsman's road shopping. Complete roadkill cooking instructions are in Buck's pop classic *The Original Roadkill Cookbook*, soon to be a major motion picture starring Andy Devine, Doris Day, William Holden, Screamin' Jay Hawkins, Anna Nicole Smith, John Belushi, Robert Mitchum, Freddy Fender, and America's last passenger pigeon.

SHOOTING HOURS

OPENING DAY: Around the country, the first day of most bird-hunting seasons starts at noon. Game wardens claim this practice has its roots in auto racing, where the checkered flag isn't dropped until the spectators have a chance to get over their hangovers from the previous night.

This late start also gives the birds a chance to do their early morning chores before the "shock and awe" of opening-day ground artillery. Depending on the bird species, these chores consist of walking and swimming around aimlessly, clucking, and quacking. Upland-bird hens check their nests to see which eggs or chicks the skunks, foxes, coyotes, or survivalists ate the night before. Adult waterfowl look for ducklings not eaten by muskies or snapping turtles.

HUNTING TECHNIQUES: GENERAL

OPENING DAY PLUS ONE: The second and following days typically start one-half hour before sunrise and continue until sunset.

DEFINITIONS

✔ Sunrise for a nonresident hunter is whenever the headlights on the rental vehicle don't work so well while shining on birds feeding on the salted gravel on the road shoulders.

✔ Sunset for a nonresident hunter is similar to sunrise, just later and with that large yellow object in the sky moving in reverse.

✔ Sunrise for a resident hunter is whenever the spotlights or headlights on the truck don't work so well while shining on deer or elk in the pasture.

✔ Sunset for the resident hunter is when happy hour begins at the tavern.

BAG LIMITS

All bird-hunting regulations have a section authorizing bag limits for each season and for each bird species. Sometimes, when they are in a hurry to print the regulations, game departments fail to note that bag limits are negotiable if an individual buys tickets to the warden's ball.

 BUCK'S BONUS TIP: The warden's balls in Maine and Vermont are quite large.

Bag limits used to be much larger, but that was when the bags themselves were larger. Take potato bags, for example. Potatoes used to be sold in fifty-pound "gunnysacks." But now modern shoppers (other than the Irish) can buy just one potato at a time—which doesn't take much of a bag, we must admit.

In Minnesota, an average-sized daily bag includes four ducks but not more than one hen mallard, two wood ducks, one canvasback duck, two hundred chickadees, and the first robin of spring. If you have a large bag and are in the bag yourself, your perceived bag limit is much higher.

Smaller bag limits also align with the smaller game bags sewed on the back of upland-hunting vests and jackets. There are a few exceptions; for example, bird hunters in Maine who wear an L. L. Bean extra-extra-large jacket are allowed to fill a larger game bag if they drop a bird off at the state trooper's house before heading home.

BUCK'S BONUS TIP: **The bag limit on mourning doves requires a larger bag. If you are flying home right after the hunt, a wheeled carry-on bag is the best choice.**

Two-part regulations include a daily limit and an in-possession limit. The latter is usually twice the daily limit. If you have double the daily limit in your possession and you shot none of them, check out of the motel before the others wake up. And if you shot successfully for three days straight, you must eat one daily limit before going home—or just let your retriever finish the meals it started.

FACE CAMOUFLAGE

The brightest spot in a duck's or goose's day is a hunter's face. Especially if it's a shiny white face, and your blind faces west.

Smart hunters emulate their favorite action figures by using face camouflage to reduce glare *and* decoy birds. If you don't want to use a briquette from last night's barbecue, you'll be glad to know that the latest pigments are grease free and dry to a dull finish. Since mallards are the most common migratory duck, greenhead shooters use a drab green to attract the big birds. Hens may be easier to attract; all it takes is a mud facial. And charcoal is the only color needed to mimic the Canada Goose.

HUNTING ON PRIVATE LAND

Given the shortage of public land along busy flyways and key upland-bird habitat, at some point you will need to shoot on property owned by someone else. That someone else could be a corporation (foreign or domestic), a farm family, a membership club, or an individual with too many fence posts.

If a bird was shot while you were standing on public land, and it lands on private property, common courtesy and some state laws dictate that you ask the owner's permission to retrieve the bird. The rule does not apply if the owner doesn't deserve to own the property in the first place, such as French, Canadian, and other third-world corporations.

 BUCK'S BONUS TIP: The technique you've used to ask your spouse permission to hunt will also work with property owners. Be humble, and make your request when they are most likely to not say no, such as when they are asleep or at the store.

On a family farm, the owner might be out on his tractor, buying feed in town, or hustling a milkmaid out in the barn. Go directly to the house; the owner's wife is more likely to grant permission anyway, especially if you bring chocolate and nylons.

BUCK'S BONUS TIP: Use strap-on knee pads sold at home improvement stores for your walk to the farmer's porch to beg for permission.

If the landowner says yes, ask how and where you should access the land, what time they serve supper, and whether their daughter is eighteen yet. As a courtesy, shoot only while they are out in the barn listening to Paul Harvey.

If the landowner says no, politely thank the individual. When the coast is clear, on your way out kick the family dog in the nuts and open all the access gates. Back at the motel, list the property on the Internet as a foreclosure sale for $1 an acre.

BUCK'S BONUS TIP: Trespassing is a human transgression: most canine hunting partners—especially golden retrievers—are unable to read signs. Dogs can also be directed by electronic collar to retrieve unsuspecting domestic birds in the farmer's yard.

Membership clubs with full-time club managers or game keepers are much more troublesome. Their attitude is total ownership of the club, with membership fees kept high to keep out riffraff like you. Members of this kind of club typically do not hunt in awful weather, so a day pass exchanged for a small bribe might be available.

Absentee individual owners are a blessing in these troubled times.

BUCK'S BONUS TIP: Signs that just read POSTED are meaningless. Posted for what? Teach the sign an English lesson: shoot it.

HUNTING ON PUBLIC LAND

Hunting areas open to the general public contain opportunities only when approached with great imagination, since the locals hog the best spots until their game bags are full. Resist traditional tricks such as "skybusting," competition calling, pulling the plugs on their boats, removing their parked vehicles with heavy explosives, or making an early morning house call on one of their little hunting widows.

Instead, try some of these innovative approaches:

✔ Preseason: post several signs saying No Trespassing. Coming Soon: Mallard Run Townhouses.

✔ In season: block all access points with yellow-and-black tape saying Crime Scene: Do Not Enter.

✔ Create a facsimile of a game-and-fish-agency decal at a local Kinko's, and place it on your vehicle door.

✔ Broadcast faux success at public locations (taverns, barbershops, taverns, feed stores, taverns) far removed from your honey-hole.

✔ Park your trailer near the trailhead and tie unfed blue heelers on leashes that reach across the gate.

HUNTING IN CANADA, ARGENTINA, AND MEXICO

There is no need to put your shotgun shells in storage at the end of the normal season. Foreign lands are full of game birds that need to be taught a life lesson.

CANADA

Waterfowl hunters understandably view the huge Canadian nesting grounds as a target-rich environment. Given the upcoming tariff wars over high-sugar-content maple-syrup imports, however, careful attention to Canada's archaic laws is advised.

GUIDING REQUIREMENTS: In Saskatchewan, Manitoba, and Alberta, non-Canadians can hunt without a guide. In Nova Scotia and New Brunswick, non-Canadians must hunt with a guide—or with a resident who likes American Republicans. In Newfoundland, non-Canadians who club baby seals must do so with a guide—or with a resident guiding an American Republican whose wife needs a new fur coat.

ENTRY REQUIREMENTS: Each hunter must carry a valid passport unless traveling by car. Car travelers, especially those in the trunk, must have a valid driver's license, or assorted homemade jams and jellies for the customs officials. Americans must complete a firearms-declaration form and pay a fee of Can$25 (US$0.25) for up to two guns and 200,000 rounds of ammunition. Dogs and mothers-in-law must have had rabies vaccinations within the last six months or twelve hectares and be tested for croup, a cough that is illegal while hunting geese.

HUNTING TECHNIQUES: GENERAL

 BUCK'S BONUS TIP: Your wife does not have to submit to a gynecological exam no matter how insistent the immigration officials—unless she wants to.

Only certain firearms are allowed to be brought into Canada. Any firearm that will shoot your eye out is strictly prohibited. Shooting road signs within 100 yards of the border crossing is also prohibited.

Nonresidents with a criminal record must apply for special permission. If five years have passed since completion of the criminal sentence, the individual need only tip the border supervisor (U.S. dollars only). If you plan to bring your dog with you, a veterinary health certificate, proof of rabies vaccination within the last three years, and a promise not to mount any local women is all that's necessary.

HUNTING: License fees vary from province to province. In Newfoundland, for example, for $100 you can purchase a mammal-and-bird permit that allows you to club one baby seal and shoot ducks on the water. In British Columbia, for $150 you can purchase a bird permit that is good after sunset in Vancouver's Stanley Park—and get a bonus nickel bag on any corner in the Gastown district.

Generally speaking, bird hunting in Canada takes two forms: shooting nesting birds and missing flying birds. Only natives are allowed to harvest the eggs once the hens are shot.

REENTRY REQUIREMENTS: Non-Americans must empty their pockets at the border crossing and have one identifying waterfowl body part available for the record book. Birds belonging to another hunter cannot be transported into the United States and must be consumed at the border crossing. Ditto for liquor purchased in Canada: beer consumed in Canada must be deposited in official Canadian loos (water closets) near the big THANKS FOR VISITING CANADA sign.

ARGENTINA

Argentina stands out as the premier bird-hunting destination in South America for one simple reason: the brightly colored birds on the beaches of Buenos Aires. If your wife is listening to you read this, go directly to the general information below.

BIRDS TO HUNT: Big ducks, partridges, doves, and pigeons. There is an opportunity to miss teal in Argentina too. Ask your guide.

SPECIAL OPPORTUNITY: Pigeons and doves. Thousands of them. Hundreds of thousands of them. They eat 25 percent of Argentinian farmers' crops; they would eat you if you didn't have a gun. The daily number to beat: five thousand birds on the ground.

EXTRA SPECIAL OPPORTUNITY: Geese as they are driven off crops by private aircraft. Ask to sit shotgun, with the passenger door removed.

ESSENTIAL EQUIPMENT: "Bird boy" to dump ammunition in the belt pouches, water the shooter, and stack the birds. Heat for the gun shoulders. Twenty-four-hour access to a chiropractor.

> *MEDICAL TIP:* If you dislocate your shoulder in the middle of a hot dove shoot, splint and then ice the shoulder and continue shooting with the other shoulder. Provide ear protection to your gun bearer if you need his shoulder to continue on.

MEXICO

Endless flights of doves are the biggest draws to Mexico. Hunters look south of the border for liberal game limits, extended seasons, and señoritas. Northern and western Mexico are the most popular regions, and hunting areas there are called *presas*. Particularly popular areas are Presa Quesadilla, Presa Chalupa Santa Fe, and Presa Gordita Nacho Cheese. South of Brownsville, Texas, many consider Presa Mas Corona to be a hunter's paradise for the "flying knuckleball" and other fast-flying, brightly colored avian objects.

MEXICAN HUNTING SEASONS AND BAG LIMITS

GAME BIRD	SEASON DATES[1]	BAG LIMITS[1]
White-Winged Doves	August to October	40 each license; 120 in possession; 2,000 in a pile
Mourning Doves	August to December	40 each license; 120 in possession; 2,000 in a pile

Ducks	October to February	15 each license; 45 in possession; 250 under the tarp
Geese	October to February	5 each license; 15 in possession; a shitload under the tarp
Quail	October to February	10 each license; 30 in possession; as many as you can stick inside a gutted trophy deer

1. FOR EXACT DATES AND BAG LIMITS, CHECK WITH THE LOCAL AUTHORITIES IN THE STATE WHERE YOU WILL BE SHOOTING. DOVES ARE CONSIDERED PESTS, SO THE LOCAL FARMERS WELCOME HUNTERS ON THEIR PROPERTIES. HUNTERS WILL ALSO FIND A WARM WELCOME FROM FARMERS' WIVES AND DAUGHTERS LOOKING FOR A WAY OUT OF SUBSISTENCE FARMING.

EQUIPMENT: A maximum of two shotguns and two boxes (twenty-five shells) per hunter are allowed to enter the country. Additional ammunition is available from Mexican sporting-goods stores (aisle 5, next to the canned burro sausages). Local hunting permits are required. Snake-proof socks, boots, pants, leggings, and briefs (no boxer shorts) are strongly recommended—rattlers the size of pythons are common in high grass (not to mention the brightly colored "snakes" in the local cantina).

LICENSES: A hunting permit from the federal agency SNARF is required. You must also have a consulate certificate, a special visa, and a military gun permit. The consulate certificate can be obtained from any Mexican embassy or consulate upon presentation of a letter from the hunter's local police or sheriff's office verifying that the hunter has no criminal record (other than a mother-in-law's opinion to the contrary). You must carry your passport and additional passport pictures for each gun permit, and for any counterfeiting planned while in country.

BUCK'S BONUS TIP: **Nightclub acts that include a donkey are not considered family fare.**

PENALTIES FOR BRINGING FIREARMS INTO MEXICO: Ignorance is no excuse when it comes to bringing firearms into Mexico. Senior Mexican officials say they have enough guns already, thank you, and remind their northern neighbors that their judicial system is governed by Napoleonic law, which states that you are presumed guilty until you hire a high-priced Los Angeles attorney related to the barrio magistrate. If you are caught with unregistered firearms, expect the following:

✔ You will go to jail, leaving your loved ones (and her mother) behind.

✔ Your tired, old vehicle will be confiscated and sold to a local cabbie.

✔ You may lose your job, and your old boss, because of extended jail time.

Can you see what a terrific deal hunting in Mexico can be?

HUNTING TECHNIQUES: UPLAND BIRDS

The most important thing to know about upland birds is that, compared to waterfowl, you'll not shoot enough of them in your life span. The most important piece of advice in this book is if you are wooing a young urban chick with a first-ever, home-cooked game dinner, *don't serve duck!!!* You'll have plenty of time later, once married, to cook duck in separate quarters.

PRACTICE

Your preseason practice is less valuable than the need for your dog to test its nose and tail. Various commercial enterprises satisfy that need.

PUT-AND-TAKE HUNTING
Hunters with young or inexperienced dogs opt for shooting venues where tame birds are confused through a variety of exercises and then placed behind flora for pointers to sniff, point, and/or flush.

A popular exercise is to tuck the bird's head under its wing and swing the body in a large circle. When placed on the ground, the unsteady bird resembles a nonresident hunter leaving the local tavern.

PRESERVE HUNTING
Upland-bird preserves are an extension of put-and-take hunting, where wild birds are supplemented with raised birds, typically in large, varied terrain.

The tame birds are easier to hit; after a season of being chased by champion dogs and missed by champion shooters, they often turn feral.

CLOTHING

HAT
Choose a fedora of XXXX quality orange or with orange trim, and with an extra-narrow band to highlight small trophy tail feathers.

SHIRT
The best hunting shirts are cut from moleskin fabric made from English-cotton toy moles and sold only at Harrods in London. The shooting patch should be created by a famed Vermont quilt maker using Mayflower rag remnants.

ASCOT
Of course the ascot will be sewn from silk made by worms that are direct descendants of those that originated Genghis Khan's boxer shorts. They should also carry an embroidered family crest (extra charges may apply).

VEST
Vests should be wax finished using votive candles from the historic Mission of St. Repellous, the patron saint of waterproofing. They should have mesh inserts to ventilate the nervousness of opening day.

JACKET
The jacket should be made from cloth woven in Scotland from a virgin lamb's first baby wool. The best have an extra-tight weave for 20-gauge shotshell

protection, with a back pleat for hunters who swing both ways. Especially useful is a retractable game pouch for small birds and small bird bag limits.

GLOVES

Look for fawn-skin shooting gloves, with the shooting finger made from a dried doe teat.

PANTS

Sharp briars and thistles are foiled by pants with tough, miracle-fabric "facing" on the pant legs. Pants for older upland-bird hunters or stump sitters have padded, specially treated, waterproof canvas facing on the pants' rear.

Look for pants with a brass zipper with leather pull strip for personal or gun-bearer use. The most technical upland pants feature special-action crotches for climbing over barbed wire that enclose posted property.

BOOTS

Upland boots feature over-the-ankle, beeswax-treated possum leather with lining that breathes as you do, wicking away moisture and odor of unimagined quantity. The sole pattern features the clothing company's logo.

HUNTING TECHNIQUES: UPLAND BIRDS

BIRDCALLS

These are the birdcalls most often heard in the field:
- ✔ Fetch.
- ✔ Fetch it up.
- ✔ Fetch it up, damn it!
- ✔ Hup.
- ✔ Hup.
- ✔ Hup, damn it!
- ✔ Dead bird.
- ✔ Dead bird.
- ✔ Dead bird, damn it!
- ✔ No. Dead bird, dead dog!
- ✔ Heel.
- ✔ Heel.
- ✔ Heel, goddamn it!
- ✔ Come back.
- ✔ Come back.
- ✔ Come back now, or you'll be sorry.
- ✔ Get back here.
- ✔ Get back here now.
- ✔ Come here, goddamn it!
- ✔ I warned you.
- ✔ Bet you won't like this.
- ✔ ZzzzzzzzzzzzzzzzzzzzzzzzzzzzzzzzzzzzzzzzzzzzzzzzzzZ!!
- ✔ Hey, who connected the shock collar to the truck battery?
- ✔ Never did like that dog much.
- ✔ Anybody bring a shovel?

Least-often-heard call in the chukar fields: Fetch it up.

BUCK'S BONUS TIPS: **Electronic dog collars are not intended for training a spouse, unless your spouse has a really small neck—or ADD.**

Magnum-force e-collars are designed for use on dogs with severe ADD (see previous tip). Before taking a collar to the field, test the different levels of correction on your wife's cat in the privacy of your own home, and—more importantly—when your wife is at her mother's.

SHOPPING TIP: **Lifetime warranties on electronic collars cover the life of the dog, so don't use a magnum-force collar on your old dog unless you need a new one.**

POINTING DOGS

The first pointing dogs used to lie low to the ground as they sniffed for a bird, and that posture is still common with pointers of European royalty and their illegitimate spawn. Pointing dogs now stand on four legs, unless they've lost an appendage hunting with in-laws, nonresidents, Democrats, metrosexuals, or fly fishermen.

Able-bodied canines point in different ways. Since it is proper to approach a pointing dog from the side or from the front, where it can see you getting ready to miss the bird, it's helpful to identify and interpret different calls, as illustrated on the following page:

HUNTING TECHNIQUES: UPLAND BIRDS

Birds straight ahead.

Birds straight ahead and close. Watch out for my head when you pull the trigger.

Taking a dump. Be back with you in a minute or so.

 BUCK'S BONUS TIP: Pointer tails lock up tight. The tail of Pearl, Buck's lab, moves in a circle on lockup—rotating clockwise if the bird plans to flush right; counterclockwise if flush left.

TRAINING UPDATE

The contemporary mania for multitasking has produced pointing labs that point to where they just flushed birds, instead of birds before they flush. This is just one more reason to fake a kidnapping and catch a tramp steamer to New Zealand.

DON'T SHOOT!

"Firearm safety first" is Buck's mantra, especially after his first few marriages. The most common mistake made by a new husband is giving the little woman the combination to the gun safe.

Hunting upland birds has its own dangers: loaded shotguns, ground cover that makes you trip, wine with lunch, shooters with little peripheral vision, and hookers back at the lodge.

The most common shooting mistakes in shooting upland birds on the East Coast are described below.

SHOOTING A BIRD OFF YOUR HUNTING PARTNER'S HEAD

Grouse sit on stumps and other deadwood, so it's only natural for a bird to seek what seems to be a similarly safe perch, especially if the perch is a member of your wife's family. There is one sure way to disabuse the bird of that thought, but it would take a steady hand, a very full choke, and perhaps a medical plan. Instead, have the "perch" grab the bird by the legs. If that simple effort fails, have him drop for twenty push-ups, and send the ascending bird into the ether.

SHOOTING A DOG ATTACHED TO A LIFTING BIRD

Flushing dogs may try to catch a bird by its tail, so hold your fire until the bird realizes it can't fly with an eighty-pound rudder. The one exception is when you've already chambered buckshot, and your partner's champion flusher needs a lesson while its owner is doing his nails.

When the tail feathers finally unhook from the dog's teeth, the bird will skyrocket straight up, presenting the classic "up yours" flooded timber mallard shot. Shoot when you hear the dog hit the ground.

 BUCK'S BONUS TIP: **Pound dogs land on their feet, while field champions land on their heads—yet another reason for a pedigreed dog to wear a helmet.**

A BIRD DOG'S SELF-ESTEEM

If you've had a bad bird-hunting season—too many birds, too many misses—don't think only of how bad *you* feel; your faithful hunting companion feels even worse. A good bird dog's self-esteem is tied to your shooting ability. If you can't perform in the field, your dog's attitude toward its value as a bird dog, as well as how other hunting dogs see your dog and its place in the hunting world, are at great risk.

In the least-severe cases of low canine self-esteem, have a friend drop dead birds from a tree stand, timed with your shooting. Or throw dead birds from behind you as you shoot. Or cover the dog's eyes when you shoot. Or simply train your dog to pick up birds you said you hit but didn't, and set aside money for the canine therapist bills. As a last resort, shoot nongame birds—sparrows, red-tailed hawks, bald eagles, and the like.

NOTE: While eagle feathers are no longer required for the Eagle Scout induction ceremony, game wardens like to collect them. Turn the entire carcass over to your local official.

SELF-ESTEEM TIP: **Low self-esteem is manifested by a lower appetite, fewer tail wags, and lethargic behavior. The lowest self-esteem produces vomiting, diarrhea, and running away when it's time to accompany you to the field.**

In the most severe case of low canine self-esteem, you simply must give your dog to a better shooter, at least during the season. It's not a bad idea to give your wife to a better shooter at the same time. She'll be looking for another "alpha dog" soon enough.

HUNTING IN SNAKE COUNTRY

Upland-bird habitats are often swarming with poisonous snakes. The most common snakes in these habitats are of the pit-viper family, which includes copperheads, water moccasins (also known as cottonmouths), and the familiar rattlesnake—a snake whose bite is worse than its bark, with the exception of the Arizona barking rattlesnake. Snakes generally avoid human interaction. You can avoid *their* interaction by leaving them alone, avoiding tall grasses, and keeping extremities (including genitals) away from areas you cannot see, especially in quail country.

> **BUCK'S BONUS TIP:** The best way to avoid a killer-snake bite is to send your mother-in-law or the wife's dog through the brush before you head through.

IDENTIFICATION

Poisonous snakes have fangs that contain nerve-killing juices. The smartest, deadliest snakes are the longest in the tooth.

Old snakes are easiest to identify; aging rattlesnakes, for example, have more rattles. If your mother-in-law is bit on her droopy arse by a mature rattler, and the fangs actually penetrate the blubber on that super-sized heinie, she may have an out-of-body experience. The rattle can be reused to call the snake gods again.

> **BUCK'S BONUS TIP:** A rattler's rattle sounds like air leaking from a tire. If it isn't a snake, hope you have a spare, especially in the high desert, where families of rattlers are known to prowl at night.

EMERGENCY FIRST AID

✔ Identify and kill the snake, unless it is moving toward your mother-in-law.

✔ Wash the wound with soap and water.

✔ Immobilize the bitten area and keep it lower than your heart—unless you are bitten in the head. In that case, say goodbye to everyone.

✔ Seek medical help except in the previous circumstance; in that case, others will need a shovel and easy digging.

If the victim makes it to the clinic, doctors administer an antivenin prepared from the blood serum of horses that have been injected with venom. Snakebite victims allergic to horse proteins should receive an antivenin cultivated in sheep's blood. The former antivenin does, however, create a healthy appetite for fresh alfalfa.

There is good news. You will not die from a rattlesnake bite—unless your immune system is compromised by voting Democratic or contracting some other sexually transmitted disease.

HOW TO AGE AND SEX AN UPLAND GAME BIRD

AGING

Biologists age a bird while in the hand. Feather length is used as a measurement, since old roosters and drakes don't have typical human indicators such as enlarged prostates; wobbly, worn teeth; or accidental farts. For all upland birds other than pheasants, the three outer primary feathers identify an adult or juvenile bird (see figure). Before an encounter with a fully choked 12 gauge, each bird has ten primary feathers on each wing. If you turn the intact wing, and the quills on

the two outermost feathers (numbers 9 and 10) are blue and soft, that means the feathers are still growing and belong to an adult bird.

The tips on an adult bird are usually rounded, with smooth edges. If the duck is small, yellow, and peeps, you'll need more than one to make a hearty meal.

The older the wild bird, the tougher the wild bird. The older the wild bird, the better trophy the wild bird. Table fare or wall hanger? What to do? (There is no such dilemma with hens, especially during a difficult divorce.)

 BUCK'S BONUS TIP: **Don't even bother aging Canada geese. Just hand them their ass as often as you can.**

With turkeys, a jake's spur is one-half inch or less and has a three- to four-inch beard. An old gobbler has at least one-inch spurs and a long beard, which explains the stumbling sound often heard in the woods.

SEXING

Pheasants are sexed by the length of spurs between the foot and the knee. If the spur is less than three-quarter inch in length, including the leg bone, the bird is a juvenile; if it is longer than three-quarter inch, the bird is an adult male. If the landing gear has been blown off, put that bird in the hunting guide's game bag.

Male sage grouse are larger than hens, with a distinctive white spine on the tail feathers; as table fare, either sex will be enjoyed by your dogs.

The tail feathers of a female sharp-tailed grouse show buff-and-black horizontal stripes, while the male pattern is lighter, with a more vertical striping pattern. The shoulder feathers on a male Hungarian partridge are more rust colored than the female's. If the central tail feather on a ruffed grouse is longer than six inches, it's a male; if it's less than six inches, it's a female. Hen turkeys show buff-colored barring on their breast feathers, while the gobblers have an all-black chest, not to mention a noticeable waddle. And male ducks are more colorful *and* more cheerful to be around than hens.

HOW TO SCORE A TURKEY

✔ Weigh your bird in ounces and convert to a decimal.

✔ Measure each spur from the leg out; multiply the combined length by ten (twenty in Canada) to get your spur points. Spurs measuring over one and one-half inches must also be witnessed by a religious authority.

✔ To get beard points, measure the beard length, and multiply by two. If a long-beard turkey has two beards, measure each, convert to a decimal, and multiply by two. If the tom has three beards, it's the gobbler section of the ZZ Top band.

✔ To get a total score, add the weight, spur points, beard points, and the weight of your mother-in-law before she takes her first dump of the day.

✔ Send a press release, with photo, to the local paper.

THE DIFFERENT KINDS

The best thing about upland-bird hunting is there is no need to get up early—unless you need to block access to a popular hunting spot.

> **BUCK'S BONUS TIP:** Upland birds live in groups called coveys. Usually there are at least two generations, the elders noticeably slowed by lead poisoning. A covey becomes a flock when you don't aim.

CHUKAR

SCIENTIFIC NAME: *Alectoris chukar*

COMMON NAME: Red-legged partridge, som'bitch, rock partridge, som'bitch.

DISTINGUISHING FEATURES: The sharply defined throat patch distinguishes this chukar from others in the red-legged partridge family. The Movie Theater Owners' Concessionaire Council attributes the distinctive leg coloring to a partridge's preferred diet of red licorice. It is hard to tell the difference between the sexes, but the cock is usually larger and heavier, especially when tumescent.

DISTRIBUTION: Mountainous areas in the western states, with sizable populations in Nevada, Idaho, Washington, and Oregon. The original Partridge family lived in Ohio until the young widow moved her flock west to Las Vegas and Hollywood.

HABITAT: Chukars prefer high-desert terrain, where they can live a simple, peaceful life near water, cheat grass, sagebrush, and rattlesnakes that can swallow a pig. Rock outcroppings are traditional safe havens; the terrain protects them from weather, natural predators, and unnatural predators such as upland hunters. They live where even the most unscrupulous developers cannot envision a resort complex.

Hunters with advanced chukar fever divide their time and attention between steep river canyons and mountaintops. There is little hope for these hunters.

CHUKAR HUNTING SONG: Boom, chukar, chukar, chukar, boom, chukar, chukar, chukar, in a looping mantra.

HUNTING STRATEGY: Chukars forage during daylight hours and flush short distances, unless spooked by a hunter. They run uphill and fly down. Groups of chukars are called coveys, and the covey size depends on weather, time of year, and seasonal family reunions. The Christmas coveys are the most colorful: each bird brings a twig of bright-red berries to tie to other partridges in the pear trees.

Chukars form monogamous pairings in the spring, and hatching occurs in early summer. A typical family includes around a dozen chicks, which are capable of flight within weeks of birth. It's in this preflight time that chukars are easiest to shoot. In Blue states, it's illegal to shoot chicks while they are still in the shell.

A solid strategy is to get above the som'bitches as they fly downhill to gather speed. You need to lead a bird flying downhill, with your barrel below the som'bitch. In the winter, hunt the south-facing slopes—and shoot the sentry first.

EQUIPMENT: Bring broken-in boots, mountain-climbing gear, shells, splints, canteens, hats, gloves, elastic bandages, a global positioning system (GPS) device, and lunch for you and the dog. Pack binoculars, flares, and extra food so you can wait out a rescue. Include a lightweight, short-barreled 20 gauge with a synthetic stock so you'll feel comfortable falling off rock ledges, and shells with one ounce or more of lead to smack these hardy rock dwellers. Remember, their pointy little heads are heading downhill, so, again, put the bird above your muzzle.

BIGGEST REASON CHUKARS DIE: Old age.

HUNTING TECHNIQUES: UPLAND BIRDS

CROWS

Crows are celebrated in ornithological journals as being the smarter city bird, identified with more than twenty distinct calls—which drives crow callers nuts. The major calls are covered in the chart below.

MAJOR CROW CALLS

Call	Translation
CaaaaaaCaaaaaaaaaaaaaaah	Good morning.
CaaaaCaaaaaaaaaaaaaaaaah	Good afternoon.
CaaCaaaaaaaaaaaaaaaaaaah	Good evening.
Caaaaaaaaaaaaaaaaaaaaaah	You look nice in black.
CaaCaaCaaCaaCaaCaaCaah	Come quick, the widow lady is undressing!
CaaaaaaaaaaaaaaaaaaaCaah	Look at those camouflaged dummies putting on the sneak.
CaCa CaCa CaCa CaCaah	I think I hit a dummy—splat, right on his head.

HABITAT: City dumps, any dumpster behind any shopping mall in America, any garbage truck with an open hold, and on top of the freshest road kill.

MESSAGE FROM THE MOVIE THEATER OWNERS' CONCESSIONAIRE COUNCIL: BLACK CROWS ARE NOW AVAILABLE IN THEIR OWN DOTS CANDY BOX.

REASON TO SHOOT CROWS: Crows eat an inordinate number of songbird eggs, as do house cats—which, late in the season, are easier to shoot than crows.

STRATEGY: Urban crows have few predators, so until they realize their buddies are succumbing to an unusual gravitational pull, you'll have a bag to crow about. The best way to shoot rural crows is when they've landed on the scarecrow, and you're shooting from inside a noisy tractor.

BUCK'S BONUS TIP: **The definition of a flock of crows is "murder." Even Webster knew what to do.**

HISTORICAL NOTE: **Twenty-four crows stuffed in a large Betty Crocker pie crust are considered comfort food in royal English kitchens.**

DOVES

TYPES: Mourning doves winter in the south and summer in the north—which is not a bad thing, especially if you are from Minnesota. Mourning doves fly forty miles an hour without the aid of a strong tailwind, which is reason enough to stay home and watch dove hunting on the Outdoor Channel.

The mourning dove is the most abundant dove, and the most widely harvested game bird in the United States. In their first few days as parents, mourning doves feed their young regurgitated "crop milk," which is a good lesson for other young mothers and their eager-to-share-everything husbands.

The white patch on white-winged doves identifies another worthy target found mostly in the Southwest. Slightly larger than the mourning dove, this bird is the second most-numerous migrating grain eater in the United States. In a large flock, these doves can satisfy their appetites as fast as the farmer can satisfy his with the milkmaid.

SEASONS: Some states have split seasons, or seasons that start in September and end when your barrels melt. States with active chapters of People for the Ethical Treatment of Animals (PETA) have no seasons; PETA has convinced birdbrained judges that mourning doves are *songbirds*, not game birds. The

PETA-influenced court brief centers on the similarity between dove songs and those vocalizations of Barbra Streisand and Yanni; if so, this is an even more compelling reason to shoot more doves.

HABITAT: Doves love corn, peas, sunflowers, wheat, and brown-top millet. They don't eat broccoli; but then again, nobody in their right mind does.

POSSESSION: In some areas, you can take twelve to fifteen birds a day and never have more than one day's limit in possession. The regulations fly in the face of the commonly held belief that possession is nine-tenths of the law—which should mean you could shoot more, but you'd have to tithe 10 percent to the warden watching you from the hill.

EQUIPMENT: The discipline to sit still is all the equipment you'll need. A good recoil pad helps, as does something to sit on: stool, chair, or chaise longue, for those difficult overhead shots. Don't worry about the latest camouflage. You could wear a tuxedo and still shoot doves, along with wayward penguins.

DECOYS: Doves don't decoy like ducks do, but a dozen or so decoys near a feeding area or watering hole might boost your odds of taking out one bird per box of shells. Elevate a few dove decoys near the watering hole, making sure the decoys sit up straight. Doves like unobstructed watering holes and sandy areas where they can see predators, so

anything you can do to make the area look like a deserted beach or a child's sandbox will improve your chances. Stock tanks are a favorite watering hole out on the featureless open prairie; successful dove hunters sit out the doves' arrival in the bottom of the tank, with snorkeling gear.

An alternative decoying device is based on the dove's habit of sitting on power lines. Construct a cross from a metal that conducts electricity well, and hot-wire the limbs (with a few decoys) with a 12-volt battery (see illustration).

THE PROBLEM

THE FLIGHT PATH BEFORE THEY SEE YOU

THE FLIGHT PATH AFTER THEY SEE YOU

HUNTING TECHNIQUES: UPLAND BIRDS

PRESEASON PREPARATION: Shoot as many rounds into empty skies as you can afford, and more.

HUNTING STRATEGY: Doves leave their night roost to eat. Eating dry seeds makes the doves awfully thirsty, so if you are really quiet, you'll be able to hear them slurping, some gargling, at the watering hole. Then they rest and have an afternoon feeding and another Slurpee before heading back to the night roost. If you've done preseason scouting, you'll know where to set up on that flight path. If you have a morning shoot and your stand faces east, you'll be permanently blinded and miss all the birds. The converse is true in the afternoon, unless the California beaches close early. Don't move until the bird is within range; say, twenty-five feet. Shoot before they see you. If they see you first, forget any lead strategies; sit back down and have another beer.

GOOD NEWS: This strategy might work for the resident birds until they die or move out.

BAD NEWS: They might not work for migrating or short-stopping birds.

> **BUCK'S BONUS TIP:** Unlike other birds, doves suck water with their bill and do not raise their heads to swallow—another good reason to shoot them.

Mourning doves make abrupt changes in speed and direction to avoid airborne predators, such as hawks and eagles. For easier shooting, shoot the predators first when the warden isn't looking. (Eagles *do not* taste like chicken, even if chicken-fried.)

COMMENT MOST OFTEN OVERHEARD IN THE DOVE FIELD: "I'm going back to the truck for more shells."

BUCK'S BONUS TIP: If you are hunting with fidgety nonresidents and their fidgety dogs, or with fidgety relatives and *their* fidgety dogs, place them on the opposite side of the dove flyway. And sit still, very still.

Doves in Argentina think you are a lousy shot. Shoot them until your barrel melts.

If you insist on shooting doves off of telephone poles and wires, wait until Aunt Mabel is done gossiping. Party lines are hard to get going again.

The definition of a successful dove hunt is one bird per box of twenty shells, and a day without being "sprinkled" by another shooter.

Shooting clubs offer released dove shoots in which doves are released from cages; some are blown skyward by compressed air, while others are thrown by hand. These shoots are most often fundraisers for a local PETA chapter or the National Audubon Society.

The most underutilized release of doves is at large, traditional weddings. These doves are thought of as symbols of love, faithfulness, innocence, chastity, and virginity; the last thought is sufficient reason for anyone in the wedding party to consider them a deserved target.

Wedding dove releases usually follow the ceremony, outside on the lawn or as the bride and groom exit the church or Elks Club. Protocol requires the expeditious use of short-barreled, open-choked, automatic 12-gauge shotguns, and leading the birds far enough away so dove parts don't land on the wedding party. Smart wedding planners have ring bearers retrieve birds for later use at the reception. They also offer, as a courtesy, a few less-shot-up birds to the preacher for dinner in his chambers.

Other conventions include the following:

✔ Doves are not to be shot in the cage or while in the thrower's hands.

✔ Shooting the first crossing pair is a good sign and a great shot.

HUNTING TECHNIQUES: UPLAND BIRDS

✔ Don't let any ex-wives handle the shotguns.

✔ In an evening shoot, mix tracer rounds for dramatic effect.

There are two other underutilized releases of doves: the Olympics, and funerals.

At the Olympics, as a symbol of peace, white doves have been released as an official part of the opening ceremonies of the summer games since 1920. Olympic shooters take their positions in the very top rows of the coliseum and use heavy shot in full-choke, long-barreled, 12-gauge shotguns. Firing is coordinated with the chaotic national music emanating from the coliseum floor.

At funerals, a single white dove is released to represent the spirit of a loved one who has passed on. As this spirit dove lifts peacefully into the air, those still owed money by the stiff take careful aim and fire. What better way to reaffirm their staying power and have the last word in obligations? The shooting is even better when a thoughtful planner includes three extra birds to represent the Father, the Son, and the Holy Spirit.

Read the weekend editions of the local newspapers for other special religious events, graduations, birthdays, and inaugural ceremonies that might include a birding opportunity. And, in memory of no-heat, no-hot-water days, don't forget the building super's homing pigeons up on the roof.

> **CULINARY TIP:** Rock doves (also known as pigeons) found in city parks make fine table fare, especially those prestuffed with park-bench breadcrumbs. In New York City's Central Park, rock doves are easier pickings now that they are invading the privacy of red-tailed hawks on expensive West Side real estate.

FLAMINGOS

DISTINGUISHING FEATURES: Bright pink coloration, which might fade in direct sunlight. In other locations, coloration results from a diet of brine shrimp. In the United States, however, the bright colors are more colorfast, perhaps from some artificial chemical reaction.

DISTRIBUTION: Originally, flocks migrated from summer breeding grounds in the Bahamas to winter in Florida Bay. Habitat losses in Florida contributed to the bird's disappearance, but occasional sightings of the migrating remnants persist.

HABITAT: Sandy, crushed-seashell, and grassy front lawns in urban environments, warm climates, with large populations in Florida residing with families whose household incomes are less than $30,000, and retirees from northern climates. One flamingo seems to attract others. Florida flamingos are non-breeding, since their plastic necks don't allow for the range of movement necessary for the head bobbing, neck twisting, and other elaborate visual displays commonly found in other colonies.

EQUIPMENT: Baseball bat.

HUNTING STRATEGY: Flamingos seem gregarious and are often found in flocks. Given the shooting bans in most urban environments, flamingo harvests are nocturnal and, for birds decorated with Christmas lights, easy to hit.

GROUSE

At the risk of exaggerating the subtle differences between upland-bird hunters and waterfowl hunters, it might be said that grouse hunters are a separate breed altogether. Grossly overstated, a pampered estate grouse hunter is more likely to walk up to a latte stand and order a slightly hot, extra-frothy soy hazelnut grande Americano, whereas a hard-core, cold-weather duck hunter will say, "Little lady, just pour me a big cup of that over-roasted coffee of the day, all the way to the top." Both breeds regret not buying the Seattle-based coffee company's initial stock offering.

Grouse hunters seek, enjoy, and mentally bronze distinguished grouse outings. These events, especially those on the East Coast, include great dogs of distinguished pedigree, handsome double guns, dandy clothing, plantation and historic-farm settings, lovely fall days followed by royal repasts, storytelling arts, fine cigars, and cognac. Fine trophy wives personally handle the estate personnel, including the pool boys.

Grouse hunters are also more likely to know their wife's metric measurements, and they are more likely to have their men's magazines sent to the office. Waterfowl hunters have theirs sent directly to the house, which will soon be awarded to their fourth wife.

The grouse-hunting fraternity house is connected, by underground tunnel, to the fly-fishing house; in the latter, the kitchen cupboard is always bare. Both grouse hunting and fly-fishing are tradition bound, with great respect for the masters, great interest in sports minutiae, and great attention to very unusual dress—much like golf. But Buck has found that it is really hard to hit a grouse with a number-nine iron, unless it's a spruce grouse.

BLUE GROUSE: A common mountain-forest bird, these loners live low in the summer and high in the fall. This means you may cross their paths while elk hunting—which means exceptional camp meat. The blue-colored grouse hoots to attract females; with this laid-back courtship, it's surprising the girls give a hoot. Blue grouse are larger than the ruffed grouse. In the Rockies, a common bumper sticker reads "My blue grouse can whup your ruffed grouse."

RUFFED GROUSE: Often called the king of the game birds, the ruffed grouse is as formally attired as an Elizabethan royal—neck ruff and all. Of course, only a privileged few knew if Elizabeth had a banded tail. (If they told, they were either beheaded or made to eat only English food; most prisoners preferred the former.) The ruffed grouse has its own species society, whose feathers are easily ruffled when you say the spruce grouse is smarter, or the bobwhite quail are harder to shoot. Audio identification is easy. The ruffed grouse's drumming—the rapid flapping of its wings—sounds like a lawn mower to some, which is another reason to shoot them.

> **BUCK'S BONUS TIP:** The loud, explosive flush of a ruffed grouse may cause an inexperienced hunter to spot his or her pants. Presoak this garment before washing.

SAGE GROUSE: Sage grouse come preseasoned from their diet of sagebrush. With males weighing up to seven pounds, the day's limit for these large birds requires a heavy-duty backpack. The males are most known for their chest-swelling mating rituals. The hens just watch, which justifies a more open bag limit.

> **BUCK'S BONUS TIP:** Road-hunting sage grouse requires more than two-ply tires. In northern Montana, it takes the American Automobile Association at least two hours to get to you and your multiple flats.

SHARP-TAILED GROUSE: This popular western bird impresses the girls in an elaborate display on a communal dancing ground called a "lek." Tail up, head down, wings spread, the bird stamps its feet while inflating and deflating its neck air sacs, all of which just drives the girls nuts. It's much like Buck dancing the chicken for the bar girls in the Valhalla Lounge back at the lodge—until he has to take a "lek."

SPRUCE GROUSE: A spruce grouse is an easy meal for a survivalist and a great training bird for a first-time hunter. It's not entirely fair to call them the dimmest bulb in the animal kingdom (remember your in-laws' family reunion) but a spruce grouse will sit still while you try to hit it with a rock. Given the rising price of ammunition, that's not a bad idea.

HUNTING STRATEGY: Grouse hunters in the East hunt in habitat best described in Jimmy Driftwood's song "The Battle of the New Orleans": "They ran through the briars, and they ran through the brambles, and they ran through the bushes where a rabbit couldn't go."

Send in the dogs and shoot maximum-shot loads in the widest pattern. Grouse hunters in the West usually shoot grouse to eat after a day of elk hunting. Grouse are found in forests. Send in the dogs or carry a .22-caliber rifle while out hunting mushrooms or tending your cannabis plots. If hunting sage grouse, know that two hens don't equal a rooster in the eyes of the law. If road hunting, make sure you cover the dog's ears before blasting a sage bomber out the window.

BUCK'S BONUS TIP: Given the thick brush in typical grouse habitat, you may not know if you hit a grouse, but a good dog should. Allow enough time for the dog to find any injured birds—this will raise its low self-esteem associated with your shooting prowess.

ESSENTIALS: Start with a mighty fine-looking gun. Grouse hunters are sartorially sound, and their firearms follow suit. Double-barreled, over-under, and side-by-side shotguns rule, with a premium on lightweight and short barrels.

This expensive attention to detail is the polar opposite of waterfowl hunters. Judging from the latest camouflage patterns, the latter don't care what they look like; judging from the size of their firesticks, they prefer major ground artillery.

BIRD DOGS: In the East, invest in a mighty fine-looking dog, with a bell on its collar so you know where it is at all times. In the West, a mighty fine mongrel will do, with a buzzer on its collar so it knows where *you* are at all times.

> **BUCK'S BONUS TIP:** Boomer technoids are now able to put GPS devices on their dog's collar so they will know where and when their canines are taking a dump.

Special equipment to hunt spruce grouse includes BB guns, slingshots, swords, boomerangs, nun-chucks, throwing stars, and—if the bird hunter is over sixty-five—canes, walker, and colostomy bags.

Ruffed-grouse hunters in Buck's home state of Minnesota take the most birds per midwestern hunter, which ruffles feathers in taverns across Wisconsin. This success may be accounted for by the fact that Minnesota has more grouse habitat; more likely, it is because ruffed grouse don't take to baiting with cheese curds.

PHEASANTS

Pheasants were successfully introduced in the United States in 1881, when the consul general of Shanghai sent thirty-eight Chinese ring-necked pheasants to his brother's farm in Oregon—yet another reason to patronize Oregon's microbrewing industry.

HUNTING TECHNIQUES: UPLAND BIRDS

IDENTIFICATION: Brightly colored adult male pheasants are called roosters, but that still doesn't account for John Wayne wearing an eye patch in *Rooster Cogburn*. (Maybe he was shot while hunting upland birds with a politician.) In full plumage and in silhouette, the rooster is best identified by its long tail. The more subtly colored hens can look like roosters if you stick their tail feathers up the hen's butt.

EQUIPMENT: Standard upland-bird-hunting equipment applies to pheasant hunting, except with larger game bags.

HUNTING STRATEGY: Pheasants' days are as predictable as those of the office workers pursuing them. Unless rousted by illegal early activity, their first daylight activity is to look for a healthy grit or gravel breakfast. By midmorning, birds head for deep cover until late afternoon, when they have their second meal of the day. (Pen-raised pheasants require three squares a day.)

Strategies correspond to the pheasant's predictable schedule.

1. Quietly ease out of your vehicle upon arrival. Pheasants don't have many opportunities to ride in a truck, so unusual mechanical sounds, especially those made by Toyota, frighten even the roosters. (This tip courtesy of the Ford Motor Company.)

2. Walk into the wind. If you're hunting with a dog, the first whiff of a bird will give it a leg up on the competition. If you are hunting without a dog, keep in mind that a pheasant smells a lot like a grouse.

3. Walk briskly through cover, stopping occasionally to throw off a pheasant's concentration, and watching your four-legged hunting pal. Hunt Conservation Reserve Program land, fence lines, picked cornfields,

roadside ditches, and creek bottoms. If you hunt cattail sloughs like those found on Buck's sister's farm, stay dry (heh, heh, yeah, right!).

4. Place shooters on both sides and at the end of the cover for birds breaking out. Make sure the end blockers wear bright-orange caps, and tell them to swat any retreating pheasants off their heads. Be very alert in the last few yards of cover.

BUCK'S BONUS TIP: Watch the weather forecasts when hunting in the Dakotas. The first blast of winter there will make you wish you never left home. Extremely cold weather will make your scrotum almost disappear; in an evolutionary context, this is not a good thing.

One large cock pheasant provides abundant raw materials to tie many fly-fishing patterns, especially Buck's favorite Big Babe Lake fly, the humping humpie.

In remote areas like the Dakotas, where big pheasants live, there will be a dance on Saturday night down at the grange. The locals appreciate your attendance, and the good ol' boys expect any dances with their wives or girlfriends to be dollar dances.

PTARMIGAN

The ptarmigan lives primarily in higher altitudes, in northern climates. Its feathers are brown and white in the summer, but turn all white in the winter. In North America, all three kinds of ptarmigan—willow, rock, and white-

HUNTING TECHNIQUES: UPLAND BIRDS

tailed—reside in Alaska (yet another reason to visit the gentlemen's clubs in Anchorage). Ptarmigans' preferred habitat is best suited for armed alpine climbers and mountain goats.

HUNTING STRATEGY: Flushing dogs work best, especially when the birds are hiding behind brown bears in Alaskan willow thickets. In such circumstances, 20-gauge shotguns are of little value, especially when you're running backwards across boggy tundra. You should have listened to your wife and stayed home to put up storm windows.

QUAIL

THE ROGUES GALLERY

Match the bird's head to the description number. The answers are under the doormat (and on the copyright page). The winner will get to ride in the scorekeeper's Buick.

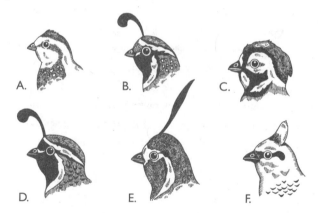

1. **Montezuma quail:** Montezuma quail is commonly called harlequin quail for its clownlike feather pattern. Historically, harlequins are similar to harlots in their lively decorations and behavior, and neither is welcome in the Mother Church.

2. **Bobwhite quail:** The bobwhite has a distinguished history of avoiding buckshot throughout the Midwest, East, and South. This proud but plumeless bird prefers abandoned farmsteads and woodlots, and being shot at and missed by fine gentlemen.

3. **Valley quail:** Also known as the California quail, the valley quail has a forward-curving, distinctive plume—predictable for the state bird of California. (Larger-breasted California quail are not found in Silicon Valley.)

4. **Blue quail:** The blue quail, also known as cottontop or scaled quail, prefers the arid Southwest, and its edged, semicircular feathers create a "scaled" appearance. This swift bird easily eludes disciplined upland-bird hunters in full-scale assault.

5. **Gambel's quail:** In silhouette, Gambel's quail is similar to the California quail, yet it prefers a desert habitat that is not on a golf-course developer's wish list. Creamy white bellies distinguish it from the valley quail, so you probably won't get this one right.

6. **Mountain quail:** This Pacific Northwest resident is the largest of the quail family, and both sexes have a head antenna that mimics the telecommunications equipment common in their high-altitude mountain habitat.

HUNTING STRATEGY: Covert action. Under cover. Proceed with extreme prejudice.

BUCK'S BONUS TIP: Quail hunting in the South is a leisurely walk not ruined by golf.

SNIPE

HABITAT: Boggy saltwater marshes.

EQUIPMENT: Lantern and a bag.

HUNTING STRATEGY: Let your friends or fraternity brothers spread out in the swamp so you can cover more ground and provide blocking action. Your buddies will go so far forward that you won't be able to see their lanterns. Bag the birds as soon as you spot them; if possible, try to take only male snipes.

> **BUCK'S BONUS TIP:** Snipes are a migratory species, so opportunities abound to hunt with friends and fraternity brothers all along the Atlantic Coast.

TIMBERDOODLE

Hunters of the timberdoodle—also known as the American woodcock—prefer to acknowledge their hunting passion in polite company, because most polite people think a timberdoodle is a candy bar. A woodcock is a diminutive, solitary, earthworm-eating shorebird. The human equivalent is a bass fisherman who left his lunch back on the dock.

HABITAT: Damp soil where fishing worms live.

SIGNS: Loose, chalky, white poop; earthworms without heads.

HUNTING STRATEGY: Save shotgun shells by hunting with a flashlight and a long-handled net.

Woodcocks and the shorebirds make dainty table fare. Their skinny legs are meatless, their long snout has no "cheeks," and their small breasts make this bird suitable for Hollywood bulimics and "slow food" adherents.

TURKEY

The U.S. wild-turkey population has ballooned, a result of effective transplanting. The population of wild-turkey hunters has also ballooned, due to the year-round need to get out of household chores.

The North American wild turkey and the Central American ocellated turkey are the two turkey species in the world. The latter's habitat is the Yucatán Peninsula and parts of southern Tabasco, N. E. Chimichanga, and the former British colony of Worcheshire. The wild turkey is the largest of North American game birds, and a trophy tom is commonly cited under "irreconcilable differences" in divorce proceedings across its habitat.

The North American species is divided into five distinct subspecies:

EASTERN WILD TURKEY: The most abundant and most hunted subspecies, the eastern wild turkey's range spans most eastern states; it has also been transplanted elsewhere. It's rumored that Pilgrims stuffed this bird with psychedelic

HUNTING TECHNIQUES: UPLAND BIRDS

mushrooms at the first Thanksgiving, which would certainly explain the Pilgrims' awkward lap dances later in the day.

RIO GRANDE WILD TURKEY: This turkey is native to the brush, pine, and scrub-oak forests of west Texas and northeastern Mexico. Its distinguishing feature is its extra-long legs—for that dash north across a border guarded by the Sons of the First Thanksgiving.

OSCEOLA WILD TURKEY: The Florida wild turkey is named after the famous Seminole chief Osceola, who led his tribe against the Americans in a twenty-year war early in the nineteenth century, and who would have whupped Disney's evil land-grab force (led by Daniel Boone and Davy Crockett look-alikes).

MERRIAM'S WILD TURKEY: These are proud western mountain birds, with white feathers on the lower back and tail feathers rimmed in white. A Merriam-Webster turkey is found on page 153 of their collegiate edition.

MEXICAN (GOULD'S) WILD TURKEY: These turkeys, also found in the western mountains, have longer legs, longer center tail feathers, and large, stinky feet.

PHYSICAL CHARACTERISTICS: Adult males, known as gobblers, weigh between sixteen and twenty-four pounds, unless their gobblers have been shot off. Adult females, called hens, usually are about half the weight of their mates, unless the tom is on top. Jakes are young males; the chicks are called poults—or when rolled in egg and flour, turkey tenders.

Distinguishing gender characteristics, from the top:

1. **The head:** The adult male's head is brightly colored. In the breeding season, its head color can change from red to white and blue, with barely discernable stars on Independence Day. Adult female heads are a drab blue-grey.

Mature turkeys are distinguished by fleshy growths on their heads called caruncles and snoods. Caruncles are easily confused with carbuncles—clusters of painful, pus-filled bumps on the hairy butts of urban office workers. The snood hangs over the turkey's bill and is considered a beauty mark, much like a supermodel's face wart.

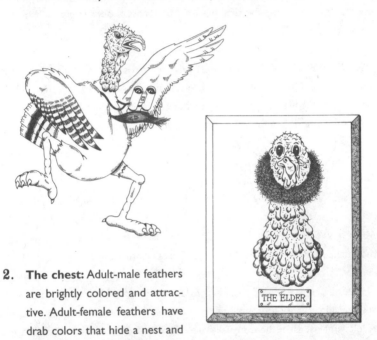

2. **The chest:** Adult-male feathers are brightly colored and attractive. Adult-female feathers have drab colors that hide a nest and mask any postpartum depression.

Adult males grow a cluster of long, stringy feathers, commonly called a beard, from the center of its chest. The average length of these beards is ten inches; they are considered a trophy marker. Buck's largest trophy was an elder.

 BUCK'S BONUS TIP: The few wild hens that sport beards are most commonly found in states that vote Democrat.

HUNTING TECHNIQUES: UPLAND BIRDS

3. **The tail:** A fanned wild-turkey tail is a dramatic courting display. The feather tips are colored according to subspecies and average about a foot long. The adult male's tail is of uniform length; immature males have a longer center feather, a sign of predictable adolescent attitude.

4. **The legs:** Wild-turkey legs are reddish orange, and males grow large, pointed spurs on the backs of their lower legs; these are used for field offense and defense.

EASTERN LEG SPUR

WESTERN LEG SPUR

Both males and females have four toes on each of their two feet. The hen's middle toe is usually less than four inches long, which makes a less nutritious soup (see "Kitchen Use of Less Desirable Bird Body Parts," page 2008).

HUNTING STRATEGY: Tom turkeys are ready for the horizontal mambo early in the year. For serious trophy hunters, spring hunts become planned "gobbler coitus interruptus."

Bring the gobblers in close, so you can blow their waddles off. Any big bird that is decoyed to a hen call—all puffed up, tail fanned, wings down, and gobbling—is fair game, especially after the strut. Shoot the tom where romantic ideas are thought to reside—in its head. Forty yards is the suggested maximum for killing a gobbler with a shotgun unless you have superior tracking skills and a week's vacation. As a last resort, jakes can be shot on the last day of a lean season. Those who shoot hens with beards are patients of Dr. Phil.

HISTORICAL NOTE: Old-timers still dance the turkey trot around a gobbler that has had its waddle blown off.

EQUIPMENT

1. **Calls:** A wild turkey has a couple dozen calls in its vocabulary, but it a gobbling tom expects you to know (and flub) only the yelp, the cutt, and their variations. Three types of turkey calls are typically used in turkey hunting: a box call, a slate call (also called pot-and-peg call), and a mouth-diaphragm call. The box call is the easiest to operate; simply move the lid over the resonating box. The slate call is the most expensive and employs a striker rubbing against a flat, round calling surface, originally made of slate. The mouth-diaphragm call replicates all of the turkey calls and comes in the largest brother-in-law models. Your wife's diaphragm is not, however, a good last-resort turkey call unless it's brand-new.

IN-LAW TIP: Do not gobble unless you want your brother-in-law over for lunch.

2. **Decoys:** Full-sized turkey decoys with photo-realistic coloring and patterns come in plastic, foam, and inflatable materials. In the spring, put out a couple of hens and a jake, and when the gobbler confronts the jake, blow its long beard off before it pokes a hole in your rubber-hen decoy.

3. **Hiding places:** Employ most any large object in the field to hide behind. Crouch in front of a large rock or tree, or sit inside a blind to break up your outline.

4. **Camouflage gear:** Wear patterns similar to your planned surroundings. If you hunt in an open field, with your back facing west, and your best shooting is late in the day, a pattern featuring a setting sun should do the trick.

HUNTING TECHNIQUES: UPLAND BIRDS

5. Binoculars: Binoculars are helpful in open country. Use monoculars if you shot your eye out with a Red Ryder BB gun.

FALL HUNTING STRATEGY: The high anxiety of the spring rut is ancient history come fall. Fall turkeys flock together, and both sexes are hunted to teach the family unit a lesson. Fine-tune your spring tactics, hunt the roost, scout for activity, and then check the local paper for meat-market specials on domestic turkeys.

BONUS TIP TO THEATERGOERS: Noted avian scientist Sven Stoolsoftnerson produced Henrik Ibsen's *Hedda Gobbler*, a morose tale of supermarket turkey bowling after hours, under the Norwegian aurora borealis.

Here are some extra turkey-hunting tips:

✔ Turkeys that lose fights with larger toms can become shy of large decoys. Use smaller decoys, or lay a large decoy on its side, or feet up.

✔ Use a turkey wing to rustle leaves to simulate a turkey landing from a roost. Squawk to simulate a jake landing on its head.

✔ Wary long-bearded trophy toms may not come in without seeing a turkey to go with the call. In this scenario, heavily bearded callers seem to have an advantage over clean-shaven callers in this scenario.

✔ Gobblers can get "gobbled out." Look carefully in all directions for a quiet stalker before gobbling down at the local tavern.

✔ Wily old turkeys can outwit both wily old coyotes and wily old turkey hunters. All three smell about the same.

✔ The ideal pattern density for turkeys is one hundred pellets in a ten-inch circle at forty yards. This technique is most effective while hunting hydrocephalic gobblers with ten-inch round heads.

✔ If you roost a bird at the end of the day, there is no need for you to sit overnight at the base of the tree. Your brother-in-law is a better choice.

✔ If the gobbler of choice refuses to leave its favorite roost, first notch the tree on the uphill side with your chainsaw so it doesn't drop on your blind.

PSST: **Turkeys on the wing, or roust the roost? That is the question. Only the woods will know.**

The following is a public-service distillation of all available turkey-hunting advice in books, magazines, videos, and outdoor channels.

✔ Hunt where turkeys live.
✔ Sit and call.
✔ Run and gun.
✔ Call a lot
✔ Call a little.
✔ Call loud.
✔ Call soft.
✔ Have a nice day.

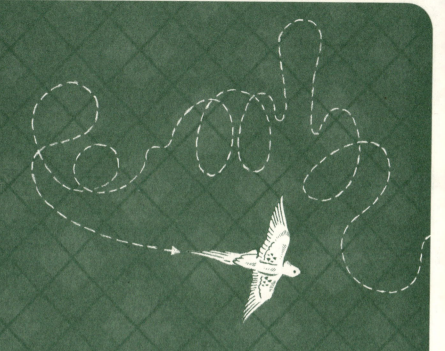

HUNTING TECHNIQUES: WATERFOWL

Waterfowl hunters take great pride in the manic pursuit of their sport while many upland-bird hunters are tying flies, reading a book with lots of big words, or painting the toenails of their championship field retrievers. The differences between the two groups are apparent even in their language ("upland birders?") and their role models in advertisements. Compare the photogenic, perky, and dry shooters in an Italian-shotgun catalog with the hard-core, cold-and-wet waterfowlers on a ducky website. To a true waterfowler, a bluebird day is so cold and nasty, the birds (and all your exposed body parts) are ice blue. The differences between upland-hunting and waterfowling equipment cannot be overestimated either.

CLOTHING

Buck's waterfowl-gear closet reveals a world that predates hunting-clothing "systems": it's an alcove stuffed with hand-me-downs, discards, and "borrowings" taken from pals' duffels when they weren't looking.

HAT

Your body is like a chimney; without proper head covering, your body heat blows out the flue. To test this theory, put on a cap, but first check to make sure you are wearing socks. With a hat on, your head space becomes a warming oven for your sandwiches. The very best caps—wool with earflaps—make you look like a Gomer, but a very warm one.

> *BUCK'S BONUS TIP:* If you plan to swat magnum honkers, a camouflaged football helmet is in order.

SHIRT

Wear a Filson or Woolrich wool shirt.

SCARF
A wool scarf protects your plunging neckline.

JACKET
Choose a hurricane-proof jacket with bellows pockets, hood, and liner. Jackets are now available from Buck's Outdoor World in Chewed Acorn pattern (favored by white-tailed deer hunters and squirrel hunters) and Vietnam Flashback pattern (favored by addled vets like Buck).

GLOVES
Lightweight gloves inside wool mittens suffice, until your hands get really cold. At that point, put your hands in the hunting guide's pockets. At the end of the day, he will have his in yours. The wallet pocket, that is.

PANTS
You'll need a windproof shell over wool trousers of any color. If your pants are blaze orange from a previous deer hunt, don a camouflaged shell before the guide sees you.

UNDERWEAR
Buy wool underwear in union-suit (one-piece) style, even if you are a union-busting corporate executive.

BOOTS
If a hunting partner "borrowed" your Schnees, any waterproof boot with a minimum of one thousand grams of insulation will suffice—unless you are in a goose pit in the Dakotas in late December. In that case, pick the toes you are willing to give up to frostbite.

DECOY PATTERNS

Duck and goose imitations are used to attract moving birds. You need to decide which decoys to use, in which patterns, in terrain that varies widely. (Then there are guide preferences, which we won't get into.) The most important advice is to place decoys in a spot where ducks sat and geese shat yesterday.

Use the following "maximum axioms" to guide you:

✔ Decoys must be clearly visible to the doomed birds.

✔ Ducks flying in small groupings require a smaller number of decoys.

✔ A smaller number of decoys means extra money to buy more shotguns.

✔ Large water ducks need large decoy spreads for visibility.

✔ Large decoy spreads in the Wal-Mart parking lot only work during the hour before the store opens.

✔ Decoys in your swimming pool will not attract wild game birds.

✔ Your neighbor's wife in your swimming pool is fair game.

> **BUCK'S BONUS TIP:** Early in the season, drakes may display embarrassing "eclipse" (henlike) plumage. Be very understanding, and set a few "sympathy" drake decoys.

SETTING DECOYS

Traditionalists use letters of the alphabet to set decoys—in particular, the letters J, V, and C. This practice is highly irritating, especially to the letters Q, X, and Z. The J pattern is also called the pipe pattern by people with a family

HUNTING TECHNIQUES: WATERFOWL

history of emphysema. The closed end of a decoy "letter" faces the wind, leaving the decoys open to incoming flights and anchoring the blind, further irritating the letters B, D, G, I, O, P, and S.

Game-bird hunters just glad to be out of the house/office use the familiar "smiling face" pattern. This open pattern allows maximum landing areas and, with the eye holes as shooting pits, with a significant regional variation:

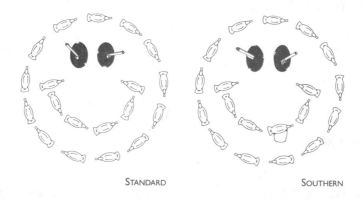

STANDARD   SOUTHERN

BUCK'S BONUS TIP: On a still, bluebird day, create your own wind with the prop on the guide's airboat. You can pick up the loose decoys at the end of the day.

DUCK CALLS MOST OFTEN HEARD IN THE FIELD

THE QUACK CALL: This basic call, crisp in its delivery, can be learned in any city park or by listening to Buck's Ducks Christmas CD. You cannot learn to quack in the Magic Kingdom, though. Donald and Daisy long ago lost their wild voices.

THE "HI YA" CALL: A friendly, cheery "kanck" greeting that starts high and ends low. Ducks hearing that call know that all is just ducky in the wild kingdom below—until they fly over cattails that go Boom!

THE HIGHBALL OR "HAIL MET" CALL: This loud, brash call is used when ducks are seen flying over the next county. Might as well have a highball in the blind. Ask the hunting guide—he always brings a flask when guiding your hunting party.

THE FEEDING CALL: This stuttering call is best used at times when ducks eat breakfast, lunch, or dinner. On Sundays, combine the first two in a brunch call. When the birds are feeding on the water, wait till they are full before shooting them; you'll save on stuffing.

THE COMEBACK CALL: A what's-a-matter-you? call, in which you fast-quack your indignation at the small birdbrains refusing your decoy offerings.

BEGGING VARIATION: There is no shame in pleading—especially when your retriever is losing hope of ever eating another game bird. Quack in long, drawn-out notes, much like the pleading your spouse's family used at your recent "intervention."

THE LAST CALL: A drake mallard always has lust in its little heart, so callers with no shame imitate a lonely single hen with a sultry "come hither and do me" quack. When properly blown, a drake's "package" can be seen on approach.

THE "CAN YOU HEAR ME NOW?" CALL: Ka-boom!!!

> **BUCK'S BONUS TIP:** Whistle calls that work for pintail and widgeon ducks also attract horny drake mallards. You won't, however, get a peep out of "championship" mallard-call makers when you ask them why low-cost whistle calls work so well with greenheads.

The most joyous introduction to how ducks call is by listening to *Classic Christmas Songs* performed by Buck's Ducks and The Big Babe Lake Brass and

HUNTING TECHNIQUES: WATERFOWL

Bong Ensemble. Aficionados in duck blinds across the country recommend adult beverages as the perfect musical accompaniment.

HUNTING IN RIVERS AND OCEANS

RIVERS

There are several strategies for flushing ducks and geese out of small moving water such as rivers, creeks, and drainage ditches.

The most popular strategy is to sneak up on the little birdbrains. Quietly approach moving water from a high-bank side, carefully glass both directions, and move to jump-shoot the birds. If you approach water on private waterfront property, for example, do not shoot any river otters—unless your little woman needs a new fur wrap.

A less successful maneuver is to have your partner noisily walk downstream, pushing birds your direction. Late-season birds blow out quickly, often flying low to the water; if trout are rising at the same time, use both barrels of your over-under for a full, more diverse game bag.

A more effective river tactic is to float, with your firepower ready, watching for "honey-hole" feeder creeks and quiet eddies where dabblers relax and quack about the stress of being a hunted bird. A quiet float with a canoe on Wyoming's Snake River in late December and early January is supreme.

BUCK'S BONUS TIP: **Attention returning military ordnance personnel: States ruled by retirees ban the use of exploding decoys.**

OCEANS

The choices are to hunt on land or to hunt in a boat. Hunting on terra firma is steadier work; even if you are hanging off a slippery, icy rock outcropping. Shooting out of a boat requires sea legs, and/or sea intestines, and/or the ability to shoot while falling out of the boat.

BUCK'S BONUS TIP: **If you plan to hunt off a point or sandbar, watch duck behavior at that location through a complete tide cycle. On the West Coast, tsunami-sized waders are recommended.**

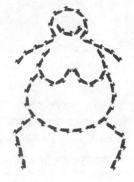

Decoys are set out in different patterns to lure waterfowl. If the ducks don't want to be decoyed the day you are out, you might as well arrange the decoys in the graven image of your mother-in-law.

On the East Coast, heavy sea ducks must be shot multiple times: while they're in the air, while they're falling, before they hit the water,

HUNTING TECHNIQUES: WATERFOWL

while they're on the water, and before the retrieval, with the heaviest load you can handle. For good measure and for their insolence, shoot the flak-jacketed eiders, scoters, and old-squaws again when the dog drops them at your feet.

On the West Coast, migrating puddle ducks need only one well-placed shot to bring them to bag; brant need divine intervention; and flock-shot diving ducks are best loaded up for the little woman's family's reunion.

 BUCK'S BONUS TIP: To know if you are really hunting on saltwater, watch your decoys. Twice a day, they will look like this.

And your boat will be in dry dock.

ATTENTION NONRESIDENTS: On the West Coast, the sun rises in the east and, if you're facing east, sets behind you. On the East Coast, the sun rises three hours earlier for those on the West Coast facing east, so theoretically you can start shooting as soon as the taverns close in California.

WILD GOOSE CHASE

If you only wound a large Canada goose, that bird will be very unhappy and sail as far away as possible. Once it lands, fair chase dictates that this large, very irritated bird be retrieved and humanely, and quickly "dispatched" to release its depraved soul. The big question is, Who is to handle this task? If you have a big lab with really large testicles, throw him out of the comfortable goose pit. If you have a pack of brain-addled blue heelers, set them loose too. If you don't have a dog, send out the guide. If he too refuses to do battle with the broken-winged monster, send the youngest member of the firing squad for a valuable lesson in self-defense.

BUCK'S BONUS TIP: For the unlucky retriever: when the wounded goose isn't looking (which is almost never) grab it behind its head, by the neck, and—in a mimic of Babe Ruth up to bat—swing widely, in memory of your fouled golf courses and public beaches.

RETRIEVING CRIPPLED DUCKS

Crippled or wounded ducks are considered part of your legal game bag, especially in Canada, where most everyone is in the bag. To avoid going to the hoosegow, make every effort to retrieve all your birds.

The following illustrations reveal the easiest way to tell whether a duck is healthy or crippled:

HUNTING TECHNIQUES: WATERFOWL

HEALTHY DUCK

CRIPPLED DUCK

Then there are the minor indications of crippledness: flying with one wing, flying blind, sudden loss of altitude, crash water landing, advanced state of inertness.

If your bird shows any of the above signs, assume it is crippled or worse. If worse, send the dog to pick it up; or, if you're in close, have the little woman practice her retrieving skills. (Have her remove her waders before jumping in.)

Some crippled birds dive and stay underwater until they think you and your ill-mannered dog have returned to the tavern. Good eating ducks like mallards or canvasbacks will grab on to a reed with their bill and try to wait you out.

AN OLD BUCK TRICK: Put your finger over the reed the duck is breathing through to force a cough and emergency resurface. Then wake the dog.

EXTRA SPECIAL TIP: If you must shoot a crippled bird on the water, make sure no dogs are in the line of fire—unless the dog is a golden retriever, who won't know the difference. Aim for the duck's head, which will be on the north end of a duck heading north.

HUNTING TECHNIQUES: WATERFOWL

HUNTING LATE-SEASON WATERFOWL

Videos produced by fish and game departments reveal some evasion techniques of migratory game birds that have successfully navigated through many ground-artillery attacks:

✔ Flying with its vulnerable head and neck less extended.

Solution: Adjust your decoys and blind so the birds fly face first into your shot pattern.

✔ Flying with only one wing extended—the wing opposite the artillery barrage. The folded wing facing the barrels protects the steel-shot-sensitive cargo hold.
Solution: Use heavy 3½-inch, wing-removing loads.

✔ Drakes flying behind, under, or over hens
Solution: Hens are good eating too.

STILL MORE BUCK'S BONUS TIPS

✔ There will be days when migrating waterfowl will not be decoyed no matter what you do. The reason is simple: they simply don't like you.

✔ If you walk in hot, humid weather, the skin between your legs and buttocks may chafe and burn. Old-timers recommend a thick application of cornstarch in the morning before you head out. This cornstarch should not be reused in the evening meal.

✔ Grumpy old men perk up ice-fishing activity by enlarging the hole, dropping in a few duck decoys, and visiting a neighbor's wife in their ice house until they can hear ducks crashing into the ice or her old man's snowmobile.

✔ Antique duck decoys bring in big collectors' bucks. Given the high demand, opportunities abound to raise money for a new shotgun. Buy a few ordinary wood decoys at a local fundraiser, put a couple of rounds in them, float them in the pond for a season, and then list them on eBay, with a note saying they were found in Grandpa's toolshed.

✔ Championship dogs have long pedigrees and longer handles, or nicknames. The handles might include the names of the canine family tree, the pet names of the current owners, a Christian name (if raised by monks), a favorite lasagna recipe, and the next show judge's private bank-account number. By the time these dogs hit the field, however, they've become three-name dogs, the last one typically "dammit."

✔ When you are not using your shotgun, store it safely away from others who may wish you harm. There are many gun safes available on today's marketplace. (If you've been married for a long time, it's hopeless to use your wedding date as the combination.)

HUNTING TECHNIQUES: WATERFOWL

✔ This one's from the Pope: eating green apples and drinking a cup of vinegar a day is still an effective birth-control method.

The remaining tips are about handling dogs:

✔ Train a puppy to retrieve in the water. Most breeds are competitive by nature and appreciate an example by someone they trust, so have your wife swim out to retrieve the first training dummy.

✔ If your dog's skin is torn by brambles, barbed wire, or other sharp objects, all you'll need is a needle and some surgical silk to sew it up. Dogs will keep the wound clean, especially if the wound is on its nuts.

✔ Do not carry your bird dog in the trunk of your car. The exhaust fumes will ruin its nose, and there is not enough oxygen for both your dog and your in-laws.

THE DIFFERENT KINDS

SPONSORED BY THE WILLAPA BAY DECOY COMPANY

SANDHILL CRANE

This North American migratory sandhill subspecies needs harvesting to save it from flying into ultralight planes and other man-made airborne debris—not to mention the messes they make in the endangered midwestern sand hills.

CHARACTERISTIC BEHAVIOR: Sandhill cranes are most noted for their mating dance, in which birds face one another, croak a love call, and then jump up a couple of feet with wings extended. A bow follows, and the dance is repeated. The ritual is similar to the chicken dance as interpreted by the Buckster at closing time in the Valhalla Lounge.

HUNTING STRATEGY: The best method for hunting wary sandhill cranes is in blinds over and among decoys. Successful crane hunters use taxidermy birds. (Guides appreciate your help in placing decoys in the field, especially your advice on where they should be placed.)

CAUTION: Sandhill cranes often invite endangered whooping cranes into their flock for protection. The penalty for shooting a whooping crane can be as high as $100,000 and/or a year in prison, listening to Hillary Clinton's campaign promises. Errant hunters can petition the court, arguing that the latter penalty is cruel and unusual punishment.

States with sandhill cranes delay their seasons so whooping cranes can crash into power lines on their own. Some states even delay shooting hours to avoid species confusion in the early, low-light hours of muzzle mayhem.

How can you tell them apart? The adult whooping crane is white with black wing tips, and its long neck is extended in flight. Adult sandhill cranes are gray with dark wing tips. An immature bird will have some brown on its head, neck, back, and wings. If they have been feeding on asparagus, there will be extra brown around the butt hole.

Here's the key: don't shoot until you can see the coloring of the bird. An adult sandhill crane has a red cap on its head (from flying so close to the sun). You'll have no difficulty identifying it if you aim at the head—unless it's too foggy, and you know juvenile birds taste better.

Old-timers say if a crane's bill bends when you pick it up, it's okay to eat. (Of course, tips from old-timers on a regular diet of sandhill cranes are highly suspect.) Crane meat is considered fine table fare by some diners, and superior fare by all diners under the table.

ADVISORY: Mother Church experts estimate that a season on cranes, storks, and pelicans will have a negligible effect on the growing number of unwed mothers.

SANDHILL SUPRISE: See "Holiday Gifts," page 175.

DUCK

Ducks in North America are typically divided into two general categories: puddle ducks and diving ducks. The subcategories are easy-to-shoot ducks, and hard-to-shoot ducks. In the first category, puddle ducks, the most common game bird is the mallard, also known as greenhead. It is the easiest to shoot in city parks, where allowed.

> **BUCK'S BONUS TIP: Moullard ducks are not a subspecies of mallard ducks. Moullard ducks are a cross between a female Pekin and a male Muscovy duck; their livers are the major source of foie gras in the United States. Also, their breasts aren't full of steel shot.**

For all practical purposes, shoveler ducks are mallards for nonresident hunters. Just tell the shooter that the flatter bill is a local variation. Blame Darwin.

Other common puddle ducks are the gadwall, the American widgeon, and the teals: the green-winged, the blue-winged, and the cinnamon teal. These ducks are called puddle ducks because they prefer small pools of shallow water, where they can tip upside down to feed. The only human equivalent to that is drinking upside down in the tourist bars of Los Cabos. Puddle ducks can be found in deep water, but a large puddle disorients them, making it easier for nonresidents to shoot them on the water.

Diving ducks are most often found in deep freshwater and saltwater. The most common diving ducks are redheads, canvasbacks, and scaups.

The diving duck dives because it can. Its sleek, aerodynamic body allows it to feed on fish and shellfish, which makes it an appropriate dish for in-law family reunions.

BUCK'S DUCK TIPS

✔ Any duck can dive but, when wounded and pursued by a big black lab, diving ducks can go really deep and stay underwater until even the game warden, watching you from the hill, gives up.

✔ Don't, I repeat, don't shoot loons—at least, don't shoot baby loons off a hen's back in Minnesota. The penalties are, at minimum, solitary confinement in a padded cell with a 24/7 looped playback of Garrison Keillor reading the margins of his *Lake Wobegon Days*.

✔ Male ducks are called drakes. No good reason for it, other than they didn't want to be called hens. Female ducks are called hens. And hens, like females of all species, talk (quack) more than drakes.

✔ A small subcategory of puddle ducks are the unfortunate city-park ducks (see "Common Duck Hybrids," following page). These escapees from zoos or hobby farms do not have the bright markings and wild nature of their original species. To hunt these birds, you will at least need a current city library card. Check local regulations before taking your firestick to the park. Local indigents successfully hunt these birds with day-old donuts and a dip net.

HUNTING TECHNIQUES: WATERFOWL

HUNTING STRATEGY: Ducks fly over, around, toward, and away from you. They are either being decoyed into your blocks, or passing by you on the way to safer quarters. Your goal is to test the theory of gravity with the motto "If it flies, it dies."

COMMON DUCK HYBRIDS

Overcrowding in urban areas and shrinking habitat on the overdeveloped fringes of civilization are producing a variety of odd ducks. The human equivalent of this phenomenon can be readily observed at any Starbucks location.

The most common duck hybrid is a mallard combination. Drake mallards crossbreed with widgeons, teal, shovelers, black ducks, gadwalls, and, where available, small pets, with an unusual preference for chihuahuas. Dabbler and diver mixes are rare, as coastal ducks submerge when they see a greenhead with its "loving" gear down and in a locked position. Noted avian scientist Sven Stoolsoftnerson's landmark study in the early 1990s identified more than forty mallard mutations, including those on the following page.

MALLARD/PINTAIL HYBRID: This common hybrid exhibits the male features of each of the parental species: the front part is largely mallard (with the light-blue bill an exception); the caboose belongs to the pintail.

✔ **Habitat:** Duck hybrids reside where species migrations collide, in many suburban open spaces.

✔ **Hunting strategy:** Some hybrids are fertile, so shoot them before the mallard id appears. Wait till the park closes.

✔ **Hybrid calls:** Quack, quack, t-t-w-w-e-e-e-e-t-t; quack, quack, t-t-w-w-e-e-e-t-t. In the rare case of a pintail dominance, with a pintail head and a curly covert butt, reverse the sequence: t-t-w-w-e-e-e-e-t-t, t-t-w-w-e-e-e-e-t-t, quack; t-t-w-w-e-e-e-e-t-t, t-t-w-w-e-e-e-e-t-t, quack.

MALLARD/DOMESTIC DUCK HYBRID: Domestic hens easily succumb to the wildness of the mallard drake.

✔ **Habitat:** This hybrid is found in urban environments where wild mallards have short-stopped due to the target-rich environment for the testosterone-fueled drake mallard.

✔ **Hunting strategy:** Wait till the park closes.

CANADA GOOSE

The most common wild goose found in North America is the Canada goose. The species is named for its traditional breeding grounds, not for a slavish devotion to the country's national sports: ice hockey and clubbing baby seals.

The Canada goose nests north of the U.S. border, and it's not uncommon for Canadian restaurateurs to steal goose eggs for their grand-slam breakfast

HUNTING TECHNIQUES: WATERFOWL

specials. This practice causes great commotion in the nesting grounds, believe you me!

The Canada goose is easily identified by its ability to shit its brains out on the greens and tees of U.S. golf courses, public and private, every day of the year. Golf course operators are experimenting with hybrid grass seed containing antidiarrheal genes, in hopes that the geese will dump their loads while traveling over the large lakes and rivers where they remain, safely out of range, until feeding again. In Wisconsin, leftover cheese curds are used to bind the bowels of short-stopping birds. Major U.S. pharmaceutical companies are studying this unusual phenomenon for comparisons with the hefty-sized bags of human waste that grease the political machinery in our nation's capital.

Tracks

Its second most identifying feature is its distinctive black-and-white markings. All Canada geese sport a white "chin strap" on a black neck and head.

While the general impression is of one large, happy family of look-alike Canada geese, there are six recognized subspecies that vary by size, coloring, call, and fecal capacity. Toxicologists divide honkers into greater or lesser categories; sex therapists divide them by sex. Male and female Canada geese, however, look alike. You have to pluck a honker to identify its private parts—another reason to remove the breast meat rather than plucking a whole bird.

Since the publisher has a paper shortage, we will concern ourselves with only two subspecies.

CANADA MAXIMUS: The giant Canada goose, once thought to be extinct, was rediscovered in the early 1960s near the renowned Mayo Clinic. (At the time, the Minnesota Vikings were experimenting with growth hormones—until the supersizing effect appeared first in the players' egos during contract negotiations.) These large sky carp can weigh up to twenty pounds, with a wingspan of up to six feet. Only swans are larger, but the season for swans on Swan Lake lasts for only three acts.

The rationale for hunting the big geese is this: An average-sized wild goose can live from fifteen to twenty years; in captivity, up to thirty years. If an adult lives fifteen years, and if the average-sized adult honker poops three pounds a day, that goose will unload more than one thousand pounds a year, and fifteen thousand pounds in its lifetime. And that's without even tasting your mother-in-law's meatloaf. A less migratory giant honker, weighing up to twenty pounds, could dump a load five times that amount. So, the younger a large honker you shoot,

the more active you are in global waste management, and the more solid a citizen you become. The older goose that you miss will, at least, be encouraged to drop its load elsewhere.

CANADA LESSER: This is the honker you shoot while waiting for the larger birds to come in. This group includes the oft-threatened, small, cackling Canada goose subspecies known best by its lesser neck meat. A cackling goose is a goose with a culmen (bill) length of thirty-two millimeters or less. Be sure to bring your culmen-measuring stick when hunting Canada geese.

HUNTING STRATEGY: Goose hunting experts say, "Think like a goose." Nonsense! If you thought like a goose, you'd head to the nearest golf course to take a dump on the ladies' tees.

Here are the key elements in good goose hunting.

✔ **Scouting:** Canada geese eat in the morning and the afternoon; between meals, they return to water, or they try to squeeze in an eighteen-hole fecal spray. Once you know their favorite groceries and traveling paths—and if you remember to bring your shotgun—you will be successful.

✔ **Hiding:** There is no need to hide from urban geese unless they have gathered around your family's picnic basket. In the wild, however, honkers enjoy a good surprise. Your hidey-hole can be as simple as a crop wheel, a fence line, a hole in the ground, behind a confidence decoy, a commercially made blind, or a large, friendly farmer's wife.

✔ **Decoying:** Urban geese can be decoyed to any urban human activity, unless you raise blue heelers. Keep in mind, though, that wounded urban geese can sail into environments that are unfriendly for gun-carrying, camouflaged shooters. Use your dog to retrieve birds falling onto church, library, and garden-club properties. Wild geese prefer birds of like feather and can be lured to destruction with imitation reality. (See "Bird Decoys," page 25.)

✔ **Calls:** Canada geese are very chatty; with them it is relatively easy to have a ground-to-air chitchat and air-to-ground shitshat. Ganders have more of a low-pitched, authoritative honk than the goose. A honk, cluck (short honk), and come-back moan is all the goose language you'll need in the field. In town, the call that attracts the most geese is "Fore!" Goslings have a whispery wheep-wheep call, but you can't shoot goslings in Canada without a guide.

BUCK'S BONUS TIP: **If you are hunting metropolitan geese, the warden will never suspect that those goose calls are coming from a CD in your rig.**

✔ **Equipment:** The minimum-sized firestick is a 3-inch, 12-gauge shotgun. Heavy hitters swear by, and big geese swear at, 3½-inch shells and 10-gauge antiaircraft pieces. (If you ask a heavy hitter why they shoot 3½-inch shells, a standard reply is: "Because 4-inch shells aren't available.")

BUCK'S BONUS TIP: **A trick used to lure geese closer is called flagging. If you use a black flag to mimic birds on the ground lifting their black wings, geese (and ducks) will think they're seeing a species reunion below. To make a flag, staple a one-foot-square black flag to a dowel rod. Smart old-timers who are hunting gun-savvy geese switch to a white flag, signaling to the flocks above that an armistice is in effect. Note to nonresidents: waving a Canadian flag has little effect on mature, migrating honkers.**

HUNTING TECHNIQUES: WATERFOWL

Why is one leg of a goose V formation shorter than the other?
Buck.

NUISANCE CANADA GEESE: In an effort to control the overpopulation of the Canada goose in urban areas, state game and fish managers now resort to relocating the troublesome birds. This relocation is expensive and not normally employed unless park and golf-course geese cannot be taught to use the public toilets.

The geese are trapped by large nets and bundled off to new host areas.

The relocation sites are usually in rural areas, preferably on the other side of the mountains. They are warmly welcomed by local shooters, who need only day-old donuts to decoy these dummies.

HUNTING GEESE OUT OF SEASON: Migratory waterfowl are considered federal wards, since they cross state and international boundaries. Any fair-minded person, however, would think that honkers that don't migrate off your golf links, city park beach, or boat dock have uncertain legal status. Until the feds issue a memorandum for these large, winged bags of fecal matter, the following control techniques can be used effectively:

✔ **Golf course:** Golf-course superintendents cursed with the sky-carp epidemic use dogs with a troubled past. Club members assist by aiming balls at close range, with the occasional nine iron added to the barrage. Wardens who have been made honorary members of the club do not consider this illegal; rather, it is seen as typical course behavior.

✔ **City park:** City-park geese band together during the day, and mothers with baby strollers will call the cops on you if you try anything funny with the big feathered poopers—at least, until their toddlers crawl through the birds' waste dump. The safest policy is to hunt at night, with nets, a baseball bat, and a supercharged pickup truck.

✔ **Boat dock:** Honkers befouling your dock can be chased with a broom. If your neighbors vote Republican, shovels, rakes, and golf clubs can also be used. The best control device is a high-pressure washer. A tight nozzle seriously ruffles feathers, and a gas-powered machine will even remove their breasts while they are taking a fresh dump on your dock.

Be aware, however, that once the birds are in the water, the hunting opportunities diminish according to shoreline ownership. For example, if your property line extends out in the water only twenty feet, you'll have a hard time getting at the birds on your own turf. It's very tricky to get a jet boat close enough to shore to ram the birds.

BEST DECEMBER GOOSE HUNTING: On the sixth day of Christmas, when your true love gives to you six geese a-laying.

THE SNOW GOOSE AND OTHER SKY CARP: White geese are eating themselves out of house and home on the northern tundra. Canadian game officials have tried to reduce the population there, but there are just so many eggs a Canadian can eat for breakfast before clubbing a limit of baby seals (see "Poached Snow-Goose Egg au Canada," page 158).

Worse, the overcrowding on the northern range is an ideal breeding ground for an avian disease that could collapse the entire population. Diseases common to overcrowding include flu, tuberculosis, dengue, cholera, Lyme disease, gingivitis, detached retinas, and, in the drakes, undescended testicles.

Once the young have taken their lumps on their first wing south in the fall, providing a target-rich environment for those on the ground, they become very difficult to decoy—another reason to coddle their eggs.

We present three solutions to the overpopulation problem:

1. **Special spring "no holds barred" hunts.** In an effort to control the population, Central-flyway managers open a no-limit spring hunt on the northern migration, with the following attractive features:

   ✔ Federal waterfowl stamp not required.

   ✔ Permission to use electronic calling device.

   ✔ Allowed to use shotguns without plug.

   ✔ All areas open, all-day shooting hours.

✔ Explosives with the caveat that the curved face of the claymore *must* face the target.

✔ Use of state vehicles to carry carcasses to pig farms.

✔ Complimentary game-warden-sponsored wine-and-cheese parties.

2. **Special hunting techniques.** Snow-goose hunters on the Central flyway use any combination of techniques, such as road spot and ground creep, driving birds toward buddies, or shooting out the truck window while the warden is at the donut shop. Anecdotal evidence about using animal silhouettes to sneak up on these geese is abundant; the most common a cow silhouette, also known as a confidence cow. These confidence decoys can be used with a "confidence hay bale," but older snow geese know that hay bales are legless.

BUCK'S BONUS TIP: "Confidence longhorns" and two-piece "confidence horses" are most popular in Texas and other third-world countries. For other hunting applications: see *Buck Peterson's Complete Guide to Hunting Farm Animals.*

HUNTING TECHNIQUES: WATERFOWL

3. Fall hunting season. Start swatting these birds when they lift off the nest in Canada, and pound them all the way down to our border with Mexico. Don't stop shooting, even if they cross the border. It's covered in the North American Free Trade Agreements.

 BUCK'S BONUS TIP: Repeat number three for speckle-belly geese.

Brant-goose hunting on both coasts requires patience, persistence, and a pile of heavy shells. On rare occasions, an Atlantic brant will appear where Pacific brant play, and shooters with a double on these deserve early retirement.

WASHINGTON STATE UPDATE: If the preseason wintering brant population falls below a minimum sustainable level, game wardens will visit your blind or boat to apologize and exchange your special permit for Starbucks gift cards.

SWAN

MUTE SWAN: The mute swan is a common fixture in city and amusement parks, zoos, and the landscaped estates of the Microsoft 1,000. Resting in its signature pose, with its neck in a graceful S-curve and its bill pointed down, mute swans need not jockey for position on Swan Lake. Mute swans are easily tamed and not migratory, which makes  them easy to catch with a fishing net or blanket—though these cause the immediate loss of their muteness.

> *"Tame swans live in parks and hiss at people. Wild swans are swans that do not have a park to hiss in."*—Ed Zern

TRUMPETER SWAN: Hunting opportunities for the largest waterfowl in North America and the largest swan in the world are contested by the trumpet section of the Fund for Animals. According to the Food and Drug Administration "spokes-swan," a key identifier for this majestic bird in flight is a neck that's  almost as long as the body. Its call has been compared to that of a French horn, whatever that is. No matter; most people in Milwaukee still prefer an accordion.

NOTE: Restoration efforts to assure wider distribution of trumpeter swans include shipping Alaskan trumpeter-swan eggs to the Midwest to see if they make a better omelet than bald-eagle eggs.

TUNDRA SWAN: These swans were once known as the whistling swan for the noise they make during rapid descents caused by an "interaction" with birdshot. It is now named for the open, inhospitable terrain called Canada. Only a few states on the East Coast allow a limited "tundra swan song," and Montana and both Dakotas also have a limited swan season. If you live on either coast, note that the Dakotas are split between North and South, where buffalo still roam.

HUNTING STRATEGY: Swans establish lifelong bonds with a mate, which shames swan shooters for their own profligate ways. It's also the reason game managers in states with high divorce rates offer a season on these happy couples.

FROM FIELD TO TABLE

BIRD CARE

If you shot the wrong bird or a protected bird or too many birds, and you see flashing red lights racing toward you down a dusty road, you have two choices: save the bird, or hide the bird.

To perform cardiopulmonary resuscitation on a game bird:

1. Open the bird's bill and remove any obstructions, such as corn kernels, from the bird's air passage. (If the bird is a Canada honker, this procedure will not be enjoyable; instead, add more obstructions to the air passage, and throw yourself on the mercy of the court.)

2. Cover the bird bill with your mouth and breathe normally.

3. Lay the bird on its back and compress the sides of its ribcage (120 compressions per minute).

4. Alternate breaths with compressions at a ratio of roughly thirty to two, or two to thirty. Continue this step until the bird responds, or until mental-health professionals secure you with a custom-made, extra-long-sleeved, white jacket that ties in the back.

If you opt for hiding the bird, you'll find that upland birds will be noticeable if tucked into svelte, form-fitting upland-bird garments. Waterfowl will be less noticeable tucked into large cold-weather clothing "systems," unless you are trying to hide an adult whooping crane. (If the warden has been watching your retriever from afar, the last hiding place the warden will suspect is in its mouth.)

BUCK'S BONUS TIP: Restitution fines are based on the estimated cost of replacement, which can range from a roll of nickels (for a coot) to your SUV (to replace a trumpeter swan). Judges don't distinguish between genders, so if you see peacocks, shoot the entire, noisy, garden-eating flock.

If you shot only your legal limit of legal birds, you'll need to prepare the birds for the table.

1. Field-dress (gut) and pluck the bird as soon as you can, unless you are shooting geese in North Dakota in December. Those birds will be frozen before they hit the ground.

2. Make room in the beer chest—using standard emergency thirst-quenching procedures—for the birds. Place dressed birds in the beer chest to keep them cool. Your emergency thirst-quenching procedures will keep you cool, too.

3. Birds left in the trunk all day are a bear to pluck (but much easier to pluck than a bear). Much like the stretched canvas that covers your tired bones, a bird's skin has a function; the plucked skin of a bird, when roasted right, is like the rich, hardened crust on a crème brûlée.

BUCK'S BONUS TIP: Don't flush feathers down the toilet in your motel room until you are ready to check out. (See "Bird Cleaning in Motel Rooms," page 145.)

AT THE END OF THE DAY

A good day afield must come to an end, which is usually signaled by the gradual absence of light.

There are a few remaining tasks to complete before heading to the honor bar.

DIVIDING THE BIRDS

The hunting guide (or the most anal member of your hunting party) will lay out all the birds on the tailgate, or in a line on the ground, for photos. Once this has been accomplished, the birds are divided for individual hunter handling or taken to a lodge facility for processing. If the opportunity presents itself, volunteer to do the dividing.

UPLAND BIRDS: Put all intact birds in your pile—the larger, the better (except sage grouse). Don't worry about dividing your chukar harvest; there are only so many ways to divide one bird.

DUCKS: On Buck's Big Babe Lake, the following ducks are set aside for personal consumption:

✔ Mallards that fly along the sweet-corn flyway. Greenhead connoisseurs prefer birds that fed on high-sugar-content hybrid-seed corn.

✔ Teal of any wing color. Eating these winged acrobats is the only way to slow them down.

BUCK'S BONUS TIP: Mergansers can be palmed off on nonresidents as skinny black ducks.

GEESE: When dividing Canada geese, choose the smaller birds that were hit in the head, fell the shortest distance, and gave the least resistance to the retriever.

SWANS: In areas where there is a swan season, claim the biggest bird. In areas where there is no swan season, place the deceased swan in an in-law's game bag, and exclaim that you've never seen such a large white goose.

CONTRACT BIRD CLEANING

Outfitters and bird-hunting camps offer bird-cleaning services. On property, birds are cleaned by hunting guides who don't laugh at lame nonresident hunter jokes or console upland-bird hunters who assumed that a more expensive gun would improve their shooting. Off property, birds are cleaned by individuals without Social Security numbers, or members of the local PETA chapter willing to share the pain.

There are two kinds of bird cleaning by contract services:

1. **Plucking:** Plucking saves the skin and all the meat for roasting. Large birds—such as a farmer's barnyard turkey—need to be plucked to save their leg meat. Small birds need to be plucked, if only for their self-esteem. Peacocks deserve to be plucked alive for keeping Buck awake.

   In a commercial camp, feathers are removed by a rotating drum with rubber "fingers." Pluckers can be identified easily by the feathers in their hair, eyebrows, and clothing, and by their practice of spitting feathers outside the plucking shack. If the pluckers also gut the birds, the pluckers could be mistaken for extras in the next *Texas Chainsaw Massacre* movie.

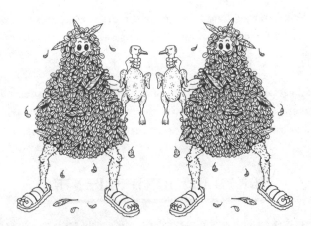

2. **Breasting:** As the name implies, breasting removes the breast of the bird. This procedure is preferred by those who shot and wish to hide the identity of nongame birds such as the first robin of spring, the bluebird of happiness, Big Bird, hens of all bird species, or a Seattle Seahawk. This procedure is also favored by those who hunt snow geese during the spring migration and by those who shot ducks at close range with goose loads.

FROM FIELD TO TABLE

BIRD CLEANING IN MOTEL ROOMS

If you are unable to completely clean your birds in the field, consider doing so in the privacy and convenience of your motel room. Think of the benefits: warm surroundings, outdoor channels, adult beverages, and, depending on availability, hookers.

EQUIPMENT

To get started, you'll need the following items:
- ✔ Knife
- ✔ Game shears
- ✔ Paper towels
- ✔ Toilet
- ✔ Plunger (most important of all)

> *BUCK'S BONUS TIP:* **When making a room reservation, make sure your room doesn't have the new water-saving toilets; they make flushing large bird parts impossible. Make your reservation directly with the motel, not with a motel-chain operator, assuring that your room is in the back. That way, you can check out without the desk clerk identifying you to the local authorities—and the girls can get in and out without security on their tail, if you know what I mean.**

TECHNIQUE

1. Call the front desk to arrange for a late checkout. Figure on five minutes per bird, plus time for showering with your girls and your dogs.

2. Unless the bathtub is still being used as a beer-cooling device, empty the game birds there.

3. Dry-pluck each bird over the toilet bowl, as close to the toilet water as possible (assuming the toilet bowl isn't being used as a backup beer cooler). Hold the bird's head pointed down, and pull the feathers back.

4. When the feathers cover the entire water surface, flush.

5. Repeat steps one through four until all birds are picked clean.

> **BUCK'S BONUS TIP:** Upland-bird feathers are liable to fly loose, so peel close to the water. Also, after a few flushes, the water surface gets greasy, so stir in a layer of a good toilet bowl cleanser.

DISPOSING OPTIONS

Plastic laundry or dry-cleaning bags would be ideal. However, in rural areas of Blue states, and everywhere in Red states, motels don't provide such luxuries. Likewise, pillow cases with a count of ten threads per square inch will leak, so disregard that idea as well. The best choice is the toilet bowl—with a direct line to the town's water system.

> **BUCK'S BONUS TIP:** Don't bother asking for frequent-stay credit at bird-cleaning motels.

TRANSPORTING THE BIRDS

Transporting game birds from field to freezer is subject to meddling state regulations and federal regulations when you cross state lines. Then again, all law enforcement officials are familiar with your noncompliance with other meddling state and federal regulations.

When traveling by plane, unless you have a note from a commercial plucker, migratory waterfowl must retain a fully feathered head and wings.

Then, airline baggage handlers can have their pick of the birds when they break open your bags looking for hunting gear.

Game birds are guaranteed safe passage when packed in the kind of insulated cooler used to transport living human organs to transplant hospitals—unless one of the airline baggage handlers needs a new liver (a likely prospect).

TABLE

UPLAND BIRDS

Upland birds provide the finest table fare, with the longest traditions—extending back to the English estate sports of shooting pheasants and poaching peasants. The diet of most upland birds consists of seeds, grain, and other natural foods in Mother Nature's breadbasket. Though the differences in taste and texture among the upland species are small, they are exaggerated by devotees of each species. If warring food-fashion factions would come to Buck's table and agree to substitute any wild (not farmed) upland bird for boneless, tasteless supermarket chicken in their favorite recipe (except cake), the true variables will be reduced to small vs. large, and young vs. old.

The largest upland bird Buck has seen come out of a camp oven was an adult peacock. Plucked clean and roasted like a turkey, this huge bird fed more than twenty shooters. The flesh was golden like a pheasant's and very tasty. For anyone who has had peacocks strip their garden and call one another all night from their rooftop, there is no greater pleasure than stabbing a roasted-peacock carcass with your knife and "cawing" in a high-pitched voice. This tribute amuses the cooks and sets the dogs a-barking.

Larger upland birds, especially the aforementioned pheasant—a royal bird, a tasty bird—deserve a simple roasting. Keep in mind that these birds are normally quite lean, so they often profit from aging of up to a week.

An adult sage grouse is another story altogether. The roasted rooster, in particular, has slabs of dark-blue breast meat, ripe with the taste of sage, ripe for use in the next gathering of the little woman's family.

WATERFOWL

Dabbler ducks are the preferred birds for the table. To cook dabblers, place the breasts in a hot, buttered frying pan or under the broiler, just long enough to sear the meat; remove, and slice thinly.

Because of their diet of clams, mollusks, and fish, diver ducks taste just a little better than your mother-in-law's meatloaf—not much better, though. Let the dogs eat the divers, unless you are hosting the next family reunion. It will help the dogs and your in-laws have a good dump. If you plan to use divers, skin and remove all fat from the meat; you will still need to cover the taste, though. For smoked duck, cover and stuff with tobacco leaves.

BONUS CULINARY TIPS FROM THE MASTER CHEF

✔ Moose nose tastes as good as beaver tail.

✔ The overfeeding of parakeets and canaries for homemade fois gras could create an explosive environment. Use extra paper on the cage bottom.

✔ Swedish meatballs are called meatballs in Sweden.

✔ There are never enough Swedish meatballs at a lutefisk dinner.

✔ A "hard-mouthed" retrieved bird is easier to cut up for stew. Just ignore the retriever-tooth marks.

✔ Swedish *svartsoppa*—goose-blood soup—cures constipation.

✔ What's good for the goose is good for the gander.

✔ Eating a spruce grouse will not diminish your mental capacity.

✔ A Danish pasty is a garment, not a breakfast snack.

✔ Not all woodcock taste like earthworms. Some taste like grubs.

✔ Polish *czarnina*—duck-blood soup—will remove hemorrhoids.

✔ One old sage grouse in hand is not worth two in the bush.

✔ Donald Duck and Daisy Duck have had their larynxes forcibly removed.

✔ The fleshy tail of a domestic turkey is called the Pope's nose by Protestants and other uppity womenfolk. Old-church Catholics use it in soup.

✔ Plucking a waterfowl is easier if you apply hot wax from the votive candles your mother-in-law used while praying for your absence. Heat wax to about 160 degrees Fahrenheit, then dip each bird several times, allowing the wax to harden between dippings. (Once the feathers are strained out, leftover wax can be used for your secretary's bikini wax in the storage room.)

✔ Housewives used to soak ducks in saltwater to remove blood—and hopefully the wild taste. For anyone who's tried to eat a saltwater diver duck, though, this makes as much sense as eating in a restaurant that advertises "home cooking."

RECIPES

BIRD'S NEST SOUP

Bird's nests have been consumed in China for centuries, which accounts for its citizens' flighty attitudes toward U.S. copyright laws and Russian ground troops. The popular soup is made from the nests of a tiny

Southeast Asian cave bird called the swiftlet. Made largely of saliva, the nests are harvested, dried, and sold to restaurants. When reconstituted, the nest is a gelatinous mess, much like another risky taste proposition, Scandinavian lutefisk. Long thought to be an aphrodisiac, bird's nest soup is a favorite among Chinese empty nesters.

An upland-bird hunter's variation on this recipe follows. Note that the freshest eggs are best for coddling and poaching. Poach the nest when the hens are out pecking and the warden is dunking donuts at the local diner. There will be no need to bring the eggs to room temperature; ideally, they will still be warm from the nest.

Ingredients
1 nest full of ruffed grouse eggs (snipe nests are an acceptable substitute)
5-quart pot of tap water

Preparation
Take the nest outside and clean by spraying with a garden hose; insert a small ceramic bowl inside the nest. Carry the nest into the kitchen and bring the pot of water to a slow simmer. Carefully crack each egg's shell, and carefully slip the egg into the pot of slowly simmering water. (Ignore any bird shapes inside the yolk.) Cover the pot and turn off the heat. Set the timer for three minutes. Remove eggs with a slotted spoon, and place them in the ceramic nest bowl. (If you don't use a bowl, the yolks on you.) Mea culpa for the yolk joke. The publisher just gave me another sixteen pages.

BEER-CAN BIRDS

A popular cooking technique for domestic birds involves shoving a beer can up a bird's field-enlarged butt or "pooper."

The beer-can procedure works best on light-meat upland birds. Depending on the size of the bird, use a twelve-, sixteen-, or twenty-four-ounce can (a tall one for long birds). Show respect to bird's origins by using a local microbrew.

FROM FIELD TO TABLE

Ingredients

1 tablespoon sugar

1 tablespoon kosher salt

1 tablespoon paprika

1 tablespoon course ground pepper

or

4 tablespoons commercial Cajun rub (Buck prefers Cavender's All-Purpose Greek Seasoning)

3 cans of beer

Preparation

Wash and dry the bird, inside and out. Rub a spoonful of spices inside and out. Chill the bird in the refrigerator while you have a few brewskies and prepare the grill. Place beer- or water-soaked wood chips (mesquite, hickory, cherry, or apple chips; avoid peckerwood) around a drip pan in the middle of the charcoal grill and add charcoal. Light the charcoal, bring to medium heat, and scatter wood chips on coals. Next, oil the grill. Here's the good part: With a church key, open the top of the beer can in a half-dozen places around rim, and drink half of the refreshing brew—carefully, because your in-laws already think you are a beeraholic. Then insert the can in the bird's butt, remembering all the birds you've missed, and place the bird on the grill, using its legs to stabilize it. Placed properly, the bird should look like it's taking a dump on your grill—which it would have, if it knew its day was going to end this badly. Cover and cook for about two hours, adding coals and chips as needed. Remove the bird from the grill, remove the can from the bird, and carve the bird as it cools.

VARIATION: BIG BEER-CAN BIRDS

If feral peacocks sit on your roof all night long, calling their fowl friends to trash your vegetable garden, dispatch them quickly and follow the Beer-Can Birds recipe, replacing the can of beer with a beer keg. Foodies call this variation "Beer-Keg Feral Peacock." The flesh of a roasted peacock has a golden color; with a straight face, you can tell your tablemate that it is a special pheasant hybrid found only in your South Dakota bird-hunting honey-hole.

STRATEGIC SUCCESS WITH FERAL PEACOCKS: Shove the beer container up their rectum while they are still alive.

TACTICAL SUCCESS WITH FERAL PEACOCKS: Shove the beer container up their rectum while their feathered buddies look on.

MEDIA WATCH: If for no other reason, shoot the NBC peacock for its gut pile of reality shows.

DUCK A LA "WITHOUT A DAMN ORANGE"

The typical duck recipe calls for quartered oranges for stuffing, orange slices to cover torn flesh, and a sauce made from orange juice, grated-orange rind, and even a "wild, tropical" orange-flavored liqueur. No self-respecting live duck savors this tart citrus fruit; otherwise, Florida orchards would be full of duck blinds. And surviving susies know their overcooked drakes don't deserve the epithet of having "fruity orange notes."

BUCK'S BONUS TIP: If you must use oranges, make a Big Gulp Mimosa instead!

Ingredients

1 large duck, cleaned and washed
Salt
Pepper
Stuffing: corn stuffing for mallards; acorn stuffing for wood ducks and similar birds
6 strips smoked bacon, optional
8 ounces berry preserves, optional

Preparation

Preheat the oven to 425 degrees. Dry and season the bird with salt and pepper, inside and out. (*Optional:* Place a few strips of smoked bacon over the duck breast—pigs and ducks are barnyard pals).* Bake in the oven for 30 minutes. Poke the skin to release the grease (or don't). Reduce heat to 300 degrees, and put the duck back in the oven for an hour or so. Serve with sauce.

BUCK'S BONUS TIP: Here is a surefire way to know your game bird is cooked. Mix equal portions of stuffing and unpopped popcorn. The bird is done when its ass explodes and blows the oven door open.

* If bacon is not used in the roasting, any heavy, dark-berried preserve will moisten and lightly flavor the crispy skin. (Use your wife's orange marmalade on English muffins. This recipe is brought to you by the Heavy, Dark-Berried Preserve Council.)

CROCK OF CROW

While nothing to crow about, black-bird meat can taste at least as good as your mother-in-law's meatloaf. Crows eat the same mall food as your teenager, but in a quieter dumpster environment. Four-and-twenty blackbirds baked in a pie is okay for jolly ol' England, but here in the more successful colonies, crow hunters prepare a royal feast with just the breasts of the noble crow.

Yield: Serves one large labrador, three dachshunds, or any number of household cats.

Preliminaries

Strip the breast meat as you would for any other game bird. Discard the remains in a mall or supermarket dumpster, to give the remaining crow family something to think about—if they could think, that is. Scavenge elsewhere in the dumpster for the following ingredients.

Ingredients

1 dozen crow breasts
½ cup uneaten french fries
1 cup discarded burritos
1 half-eaten soft pretzel
⅓ pound kung pao chicken
1½ cups of Orange Julius, original flavor
Salt, pepper, and monosodium glutamate (MSG) to taste

Preparation

Place ingredients in a Crock-Pot. Replicate a dumpster baking on a hot summer day by cooking the crow stew on low heat for five to six hours.

INTERNATIONAL TRAVEL NOTE: There is no hunting season for the big black birds that loiter on the grounds of the Tower of London. But that doesn't rule out throttling one while your hunting partner is distracting the boys in those goofy beefeater outfits.

ADDENDUM TO INTERNATIONAL TRAVEL NOTE: Unless you're close enough to smell a guard's breath, it's hard to tell that a gin mill is sponsoring the tourist exhibit and stocking the employee cafeteria with product.

POACHED SNOW-GOOSE EGG AU CANADA

In the overcrowded nesting areas of the Great Plains region of the Great White North (also known as Canada), poaching eggs from the nests of white geese is now quietly encouraged by the Royal Canadian Mounted Police. It is feared that these sky carp are eating themselves out of house and home, and that they are highly susceptible to bird diseases such as avian flu and gingivitis—not to mention whooping cough carried by the whooping crane.

Resident Canadians are allowed to take up to three eggs each morning for their omelets. Francophiles from Quebec are allowed to take as many eggs as they need to cover the prime minister's car.

Yield: Serves two.

Ingredients
4 snow-goose eggs
1 tablespoon sherry vinegar
Salt

Preparation

Crack each egg into separate small bowls (ignore any baby-bird shapes). Bring about four inches of water to boil in a small pot. Add vinegar and a pinch of salt to the water. Carefully tilt individual eggs into the water. Cover and turn off heat. Let stand for three minutes. Remove poached eggs with a slotted spoon, and serve on buttered toast.

TURDUCKEN

This all-inclusive game-bird recipe that suits a mixed-game bag was first popularized by a Cajun chef of great renown and girth. The original turducken was made from domestic birds: a chicken stuffed inside a duck; the duck in turn stuffed inside a turkey. Each bird was boned, surrounded by a stuffing that complemented its bland flavor, and then reassembled and trussed for the oven.

Game birds offer the greatest stuffing opportunities. A standard wild turducken could consist of a prairie chicken stuffed inside a large mallard, stuffed inside a wild turkey. A "duckducken" could be a duckling stuffed inside a teal, stuffed inside a mallard.

Other suggestions include the following:
✔ Turgoosen
✔ Turgrousen
✔ Pheasducken
✔ Pheasquailen
✔ Pheastimberdoodlen
✔ Peacockadoodledooen

Ingredients

Your favorite seasonings

Your favorite stuffing

Your favorite 3 feet of butcher twine

Preparation

Bone the birds and pound flat. Butterfly all of the legs. Lay the largest bird skin side down on a table or cutting board, cover with seasonings and your favorite stuffing (place in the legs too). Lay the second-largest bird atop the first bird, and cover with the second stuffing (in the legs too). Lay the last bird on top, and stuff with the corresponding favorite stuffing. Pull the lower skin up and around the stack and sew the ends together with butcher twine.

At the same time, repair skin tears and holes from a shotshell encounter. The reassembled bird will look like a piece of medical experiment, so try to shape it in a more familiar pose before the pregnant women return to the kitchen. Cover with foil, and roast at 250 degrees, basting in own juices until internal temperature reaches 125–130 degrees. Remove the foil and the brown skin. Make gravy from pan drippings. Bon(less) appetit!

 BUCK'S BONUS TIP: The reason people feel so sleepy after eating turkey is the same reason there is a couch in front of the TV.

RECIPE FOR WORLD PEACE

Ingredients

1 reclaimed wetland
Several game birds (mallards, pheasants, geese—anything but mergansers)
Much less work
Hunting dogs that age and live as well and as long as you do
Hunting partners that age and live as well and as long as you do

Preparation

Scrape the vacation condos and golf links from what used to be prime bird territory. Add bulrushes and cattails for color. Set the game birds loose to go forth, be fruitful, and multiply. Stir in paid leave from dull job during hunting season. Season with hunting dogs and hunting partners. Garnish with camo gear and shotgun shells. Load the breech and serve. Let the peace begin.

MISCELLANEOUS

This section is added at the behest of the publisher, who would like this book to be the last word on the subject.

THE SECOND COLLECTION OF THE MOST FREQUENTLY ASKED QUESTIONS ABOUT BIRDS AND BIRD HUNTING

1. *I work for the county but want to fly like an eagle, to the sea; fly like an eagle, let my spirit carry me. I want to fly like an eagle, till I'm free, but time keeps on slippin', slippin', slippin' into the future!*
   Fly just a little closer.

2. *I am right-handed but left-eye dominant. My question, Buck, is this: do these Filson tin-cloth pants make my ass look too big?*
   Yes.

3. *My sporting-clays club has a no-drug policy. I shoot better after taking the little blue pill, if you know what I mean.*
   That's a hard question. If you shoot better for more than four hours, call your doctor.

4. *We have no open season on swans where I live. What happens if I shoot an Ugly Duckling?*
   If you can get a clear shot around those damn ballerinas, the shooting on Swan Lake is not bad.

5. *My wife is "old church" Catholic, so for her, sex is for procreation, not recreation. Is there a season on storks?*
   Yes. This was covered in the *Row v. Wade* decision, section IV: Setting Up Decoys, with or without a Boat.

MISCELLANEOUS

6. *Did you know Donald Duck had a twin sister? Her name is Della, and she had Huey, Dewey, and Louie. Most ducks have more offspring, but you know how Goofy things are at the Magic Kingdom. I'll bet that damn skunk, Pepé Le Pew, ate the other eggs.*
No. I do too.

7. *You put your right foot in, you put your right foot out, you put your right foot in and you shake it all about. You do the hokeypokey and you turn yourself around. That's what it's all about!*
Stay turned around. This pokey is about to get very hokey. Hey, boys, we gots a live one!

8. *My wife's favorite wedding song was "The Wind beneath My Wings." Since we've been married, though, her night refrain is more like "The Wind beneath My Sheets." Does Beano come in a suppository form?*
Yes: small, medium, large, and Italian sizes.

9. *How come woodpeckers don't get headaches?*
Peckers with headaches take sexual politics to a new level. Leave it alone.

10. *Why do they call a male turkey a tom?*
Because they are not a hen.

11. *Ole Oleoleoverson here, Buck. Know why we live longer in North Dakota? It's because it takes us a very long time to figure out why we live here at all.*
People live even longer in South Dakota, you know.

12. *Dr. Philistine says it's not wise to go hunting so soon after my divorce.*
At least one fat, noisy hen is allowed in your daily game bag.

13. *Buck, if I don't get a new shotgun this year, have the terrorists won?*
Yes.

14. *Hey, big guy. In dog years, I'm only ten years old, and I still can't lick my own balls.*
The Y offers a yoga class for seniors.

15. *Buck, those spots just won't come out. I've tried everything. What did you sit in, anyway? Love, Mom.*
Mom, call me on my private line with this stuff, OK?

COOTS UNLIMITED AND FOREVERMORE

MISSION
Our mission is the nonpreservation of existing coot habitat, and the nonexpansion of core coot habitat and coot conservation. We are dedicated to raising the self-esteem of waterfowlers who shoot a coot, and retrievers who don't know any better.

ANNUAL MEMBERSHIP
Annual membership includes a full year of no new magazines (no six issues), plus no membership card, and no hard-to-remove auto decals.

LIFETIME MEMBERSHIP
Lifetime membership includes a lifetime promise of no new magazines, plus no membership card, no certificate, no decals, no caps, no knives, and no lapel pins.

SPONSOR-LEVEL MEMBERSHIP
Sponsor-level membership includes the lifetime-membership benefits, plus no

MISCELLANEOUS

UNLIMITED & FOREVERMORE

artwork of coots, in full color with matching stamp, and no chapter dinners to meet other old coots.

SENIOR/VETERAN MEMBERSHIP
Senior/Veteran-level membership includes all sponsor-level benefits plus no notice of nonrenewal membership, and no holiday greeting cards with no return-address labels.

PAYMENT PLANS
All of the above no-costs can be spread over three years.

NONMEMBERSHIP APPLICATION

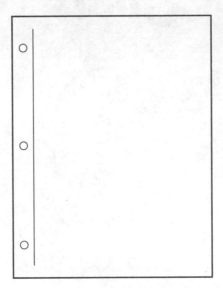

BIRD BANDING

The practice of placing identification bands on migratory birds has a long history. Roman foot soldiers tied threads on swallows' legs, and early Chinese land barons marked their falcons and concubines with owner information. The first record of a metal bird band was on Henry IV's peregrine falcon. Henry IV preceded Henry V, one of the first royal alcoholics. (There is scant information on Henry the Half-Gallon.)

John James Audubon is reported to have banded the first bird in North America, to track phoebes with silver cords. Around the turn of the nineteenth century, a Danish schoolteacher put aluminum rings with his name and address on several bird species in hopes the birds would be returned (and, more importantly, that he could find a date for the Saturday-night clog dance).

BUCK'S BONUS TIP: Today's game-bird bands often include sayings by the Chinese pop-culture fortune-cookie philosopher Sum Yung Duk, including "Duck when in-law shoot."

Banding is controlled by the same ambiguous migratory-bird treaty that tells you when to stop shooting. Banders must have a permit, and they must show they can handle birds safely, without sneaking a couple for the table. From more-or-less reliable sources, we know that drakes are banded on the left leg, and hens on the right. Republican volunteers ring the necks of any bird of uncertain parentage and/or gender. Bands are sized according to species: small bands for small and bulimic birds; large bands for large birds, small domestic pets, and women less than five feet, six inches tall.

BAND BLING

Successful waterfowl-hunting guides decorate their call lanyards with bird bands, and the most successful guides wear band necklaces to encourage higher client tips.

BUCK'S BONUS TIP: If you shoot a banded bird, there is no need for the guide to send it to someplace back East for recording.

A FLOCK OF CONTEMPORARY BUSINESS LESSONS

(OR, WHAT WE CAN LEARN FROM WILD GEESE)

✔ Geese in the rear of the formation honk to keep the forward birds moving.
   Lesson: Back-office employees blab too much. There is a reason they are back-office employees. Ignore them—or better yet, shoot them.

✔ When a goose falls away from the formation, others will fall out to look for the missing bird.
Lesson: This birdbrained loyalty has no place during hunting season—or any season, for that matter, especially in today's office settings. Shoot these followers too.

✔ When the lead goose in a formation gets tired, it slips back, and another goose takes its place.
Lesson: Leaders must rest too. Shoot them when they do. It's a good strategy for the upwardly mobile.

✔ When a goose flaps its wings, it creates an updraft for those behind it.
Lesson: There are always slackers who will coast on your accomplishments. Shoot them too.

✔ When a goose falls out of formation, it's much harder to fly.
Lesson: In today's corporate environment, you will be shot before retirement, so shoot them first.

✔ Geese form lifelong relationships and stable family environments.
Lesson: Relationships in our throwaway pop culture are fragile, so shoot the irrelevant role-model pair.

✔ Geese have the ability to turn everything they consume into a steaming, supersized pile of shit.

Lesson: If this ability reminds you of your boss (which it should), shoot him or her too.

GUIDE TO TIPPING

At Buck's Lodge in northern Minnesota, exceptional gratuities reward the exceptional service. The bird-hunting service starts with a gentle wake-up call by the girls from the massage parlor, and it ends with a full-body massage by the second shift, "with happy ending."

Tipping is a conundrum for many, especially for those who have no idea what a conundrum is. Big-game hunters tip from 5 to 15 percent of the total fee, and that tip can be split in many different ways: all to the selfish hunting guide, all to the hunting guide with hopes of further distribution to the other camp help (such as the cook, the packer, and the Las Vegas hookers who could make it), or all to the owner for his distribution to his wife, a known spendthrift. Guides are not supposed to use tips to make ends meet, so a gratuity that allows them to buy their sweetheart a new cotton dress is appreciated.

Restaurant tipping can be used as model behavior. The norm is 15 percent, easily reaching 20 percent if the waitress takes off her clothes, or 30 percent if it's best she left her clothes on.

BUCK'S BONUS TIP: If you don't tip on this trip, and you return to the same camp on your next trip, expect to see the village idiot and his blind retriever take you afield.

Bird-hunting fees are not as formidable as big-game fees. An average, fully guided day will be in the $350 range, and 10 percent of that barely covers the cost of a box of nontoxic shells.

What follows are some general guidelines.

GENERAL GUIDELINES

If your guide is driving a newer vehicle than yours, ask if he needs help carrying the decoys.

UPLAND-HUNTING GUIDELINES

Upland-bird hunters are the most self-reliant of the game-bird hunters. Where they don't know the terrain, they appreciate an overview of the territory before setting the dogs loose. If they don't have a dog, a guide or dog handler and estate dogs provided by the camp are essential equipment.

FOR THE TERRAIN GUIDE: If the birds are where this person says they are, and you plan to return, a cash tip is in order. A sawbuck (ten-dollar bill) will get you back in; if the guide is a barbershop regular, offer to pay for a shoeshine. If the birds were there and you weren't, he should have told you the birds were fast; all he deserves is a large russet potato or several lumps of coal.

FOR THE PARTICIPANT GUIDE: An average tip is $25–$50 a day, unless he shoots better than you; then those amounts should be given in some worthless international currency.

FOR THE DOG: Upland birds are notoriously high-strung, so anything that acts as a sedative and can be tucked into a soft biscuit is in order. If you missed birds, a mild "dog antidepressant" is in order.

WATERFOWL-HUNTING GUIDELINES

Waterfowl guides work much harder than upland-bird guides. They scout daily, put out great decoy spreads, and endure huge variables in weather. Worst of all, they listen to tired nonresident jokes all day in the duck or goose blind.

FOR THE PARTICIPANT GUIDE: At Buck's base camp in northern Minnesota, the most senior guides have received many types of gratuities; subway tokens

MISCELLANEOUS

from New Yorkers, keys to the family farm in North Dakota, a fifty-five-gallon drum of maple syrup from Canadians, and the only fourteen-year-old virgin in Arkansas. Consider giving a bonus tip for guides who call well. Withhold this bonus if the guide falls asleep, laughs at your shooting, or dies in the blind.

FOR THE DOG: Waterfowl dogs work very hard for their money. The best tip they can receive is some special "loving" (that is, properly scratching the dog's nuts) when the owner isn't looking.

BUCK'S BONUS TIP: If you happen to shoot the guide's dog accidentally, extra tipping is recommended—at least while you are within the guide's shotgun range. If the dog is only wounded, offer to pay the vet bills. If the dog is dead, common courtesy dictates a replacement stipend.

DOG-REPLACEMENT STIPENDS, BY BREED

Breed	*Stipend*
Labrador retriever	$505
Chesapeake Bay retriever	$500
Dachshund	$499
Setter	$495
German shorthaired pointer	$450
Golden retriever	Can$5

GRAND-SLAM BIRD HUNTING

In every sporting endeavor, there is a competition to excel in all categories. In bird hunting, the race for a "grand slam": to harvest all types of one bird species or subspecies in a fixed amount of time.

Upland-bird hunters—in particular, the eastern grouse hunters who belong to Boston-based, supersecret Skull and Crossed-Boners Society—have initiated their own supersecret woodcock grand slam. To win, an entire family unit of woodcocks must be taken in one encounter: an adult male (cock), an adult female (hen), and at least three chicks (babies).

To a turkey hunter, a grand slam includes all the subspecies. A recently added supersized grand slam adds at least one domestic turkey taken from a farmer's front yard. Fair chase rules apply—no shooting inside the turkey barn. Extra points are awarded for the taking of a domesticated heritage turkey, and points are deducted if the turkey has supermarket markings.

Duck hunters rarely aspire to a grand-slam competition because there are so many species (so little time, so many shells). Those who hunt Canada honkers celebrate a grand slam at the nineteenth hole if they've taken one giant bird pooper off of each of the preceding eighteen holes.

INCONVENIENT TRUTHS

✔ Beer contains amino acids—important protein building blocks for maintaining strong bodies.

✔ Not every Canadian brewery uses recovered toilet water.

✔ Studies show that those who enjoy a glass of cold beer regularly are more well-rounded individuals.

MISCELLANEOUS

✔ One liter of beer supplies almost half the daily requirement of niacin—whatever niacin is.

✔ Beer contains all of the B vitamins. Vitamins A and C are in the beer nuts.

HOLIDAY GIFTS

Every year, exceptional holiday packages are delivered by specially selected carriers. This was certainly true pre-FedEx years ago in northern Minnesota, when a chosen game bird braved significant winter elements for a special December delivery to a Norwegian pioneer family on Big Babe Lake.

The red cap of the "stork," or sandhill crane, was a happy holiday flourish, and a reminder that good things come in unexpected packages.

ABRIDGED AFTERWORD

"What I hate about writing is the paperwork."—*Peter De Vries*
"Ditto."—*Buck*

MISCELLANEOUS

UNABRIDGED AFTERWORD

In a world that lurches toward impossible complexity, both real and imagined, game-bird hunting can provide significant relief. The pleasures are simple—if you remove all the built-in speed bumps in a day afield. If you ignore what the "experts" say about the best guns, shells, apparel, boots, dogs, and field conditions, and the expected number and kinds of birds, trophies, and weather, your day will be relaxed and superb. Trust your instincts. Trust Sourdough, Buck, and Dorothy, the hunting pig. A good day game-birding will make you a better friend, parent, spouse, and—most importantly—a better you.

APPENDIX: BIRDBRAINED QUOTATIONS

When you have shot one bird flying, you have shot all birds flying. Damn, that's nicely worded. I should write that down.
—*Ernest Hemingway, uncollected notes, 1986*

I'm glad I died before sporting clays. I'd never have been able to keep my trap shut.
—*Annie Oakley,* Posthumous Recollections, *1955*

The color of my mother-in-law's meatloaf is not found in nature.
—*Aldo Leopold,* A Sandbox Almanac, *1952*

I don't have a clue why any caged bird sings.
—*Maya Angelooloo, on the publisher's cutting-room floor*

Brokeback Mountain was our most difficult mount on our trek West.
—*Meriwether Lewis and William Clark,* The Secret Journals of Lewis and Clark, *1806*

Where did all this chick lit come from?
—*Henry David Thoreau,* Walden Books, *2005*

If it walks like a duck and swims like a duck and quacks like a duck, take it!!
—*Buck "Buck" Peterson, as told to a hunting pal, yesterday*

If it flies, it dies.
—*Anonymous*

This book is for the birds.
—*No-so-anonymous*

APPENDIX

Buck "Buck" Peterson in front of his duck-plucking shack near the Great Boot-Sucking Mud and Cattail Marsh on the north end of Big Babe Lake. J. Angus "Sourdough" McLean is standing to Buck's left (your right if you are left-handed) and is much taller in person. The National Boom and Crock-Pot Society has applied for national historic designation for this log cabin built by Buck's Norwegian ancestors, in particular, Sven Stoolsoftenerson, translator of the Old Nordic Lutefisk Legends. A skunkweed bouquet is placed in a gold-foil-wrapped mason jar in his honor on Grunnlovsdag, more commonly known as Sytende Mai, or the day the taverns opened late. More meaningful donations are encouraged and eagerly accepted at www.buckpeterson.com.

GET THE COMPLETE BUCK PETERSON'S HUNTING TRILOGY!

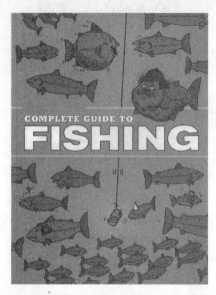

Buck Peterson's Complete Guide to Fishing
6 x 8 inches • 192 pages

Buck Peterson's Complete Guide to Deer Hunting
6 x 8 inches • 176 pages

Available from your local bookstore, or order direct from the publisher:

TEN SPEED PRESS

PO Box 7123, Berkeley, CA 94707
800-841-BOOK • fax 510-559-1629
www.tenspeed.com • order@tenspeed.com